INCONVENIENT FACTS

The science that Al Gore doesn't want you to know

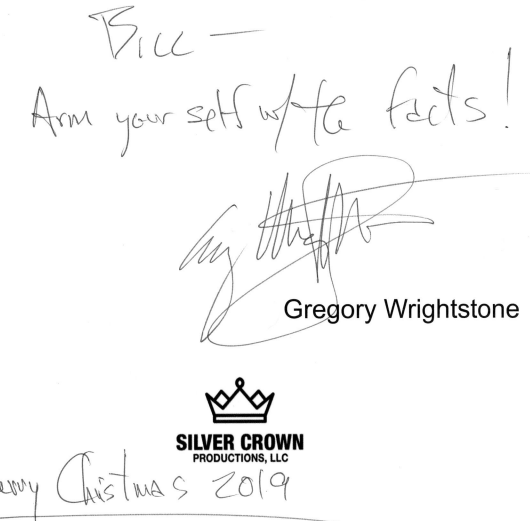

Bill —

Arm yourself w/ the facts!

Gregory Wrightstone

♔
SILVER CROWN
PRODUCTIONS, LLC

Merry Christmas 2019

Silver Crown Productions, LLC

Cover design by Darren J. Miller

ISBN: 9781545614105
LCCN: 2017952745

Website: inconvenientfacts.xyz

In memory of our son,

Zachary Daniel Wrightstone,

September 14, 1988 – February 2, 2017

Taken too soon

And dedicated to our granddaughter

Chloe Choi

born April 27, 2017

In the hope that she will grow up in a rational world

One life ends and another begins

Acknowledgments

Many thanks to the colleagues who made this book possible. Though they had diverse talents, they shared my goal of finding the truth and presenting the facts, science and data in a clear and lucid manner.

The generous contribution of time and linguistic talent from Gordon Tomb was crucial to the finished product. His wordsmithing of my sometimes-inelegant phrasing certainly made this a much more readable and sensible work. Not long into the process he told me "Greg, I had suspected for years that we were being lied to about this, but I had no idea just how pervasive it really was." At that point, he was hooked.

It was a pleasure and a joy to bring Christopher Monckton of Brenchley onto the editing team. His contributions were impactful and greatly improved the book via additions of his technical knowledge and his insight into the political machinations promoting the "party line."

Robert Burger provided great help in formatting and excellent improvements in the figures. Others providing an assist with editing and graphics were Christopher Humphrey, Justin Skaggs, Sarah Hart and Alison Kissel.

It is not entirely certain that this book would have been completed without the support and encouragement of my brother, Bob Wrightstone. He always provided an honest assessment to keep me on track with my goal of reaching the common man. In

writing a book dealing with scientific matters, it is all too easy to go "deep in the weeds" on the technical aspects and Bob was not afraid to remind me of that fact when I strayed from my goal.

Special thanks for design help and moral support to dear friends Jeff and Gwen Steigerwalt. Their help and backing of the project were crucial to its success.

The patience and support of my wife Julia were remarkable and for that I am grateful.

Special thanks to Lucy the Cat who kept me company and never once complained… Well, maybe once.

Foreword

Great is truth and mighty above all things—even in climate science

By The Viscount Monckton of Brenchley

The Roman poet Virgil wrote of the scientist: "*Felix qui potuit rerum cognoscere causas:* "Happy the one who finds the why of things." Science was originally known in the West as *philosophia naturalis*—the love of the nature of wisdom that is love of the wisdom of nature. The noble philosophical mission of "the seeker after truth", as the Iraqi mathematician and empiricist al-Haytham beautifully described the scientist, was to discern what is so in nature and why it is so, and to answer the question of the Greek philosopher Anaximander: how to distinguish what *is* from what *is not*?

The objective of the endeavors of the man of science, then, is precisely that of the man of religion: to discern the truth. Jesus Christ—the unsuccessful and yet ultimately triumphant defendant in history's most celebrated show trial—declared His mission thus: "To this end was I born, and for this cause came I into the world, that I should bear witness unto the truth." There, in a sentence, is a noble mission for every true natural philosopher to adopt as his own. Too many climate scientists have abandoned that mission, and they have done so at great cost to the reputation of science itself.

Pontius Pilate's reply to the defendant was the great question that underlies all genuine scientific questions: "What is the truth?" There, before him, was the One who could have given the answer, but, notoriously, Pilate did not stay for it.

Similarly do today's governing elite respond when they are confronted with the Inconvenient Facts piled upon Inconvenient Facts in this book, establishing that global warming is not occurring at anything like the predicted rate, that the succession of exotic natural disasters luridly foretold by failed climate models are not happening, and that the cost of solving non-existent man-made global warming is orders of magnitude greater than the far lesser cost of doing nothing today and adapting to warmer weather—if ever it comes.

They close their ears to the truth and walk away. Hear no truth, see no truth, speak no truth.

The lavishly-funded clique of totalitarian pseudo-scientists who crafted the scare of scares and then peddled the scam of scams—Professor Mörner justly calls climate alarmism "the greatest lie ever told"—bear witness not unto the truth but unto the Party Line, which they have branded as "the overwhelming scientific consensus"; a consensus which, as Mr. Wrightstone explains with admirable lucidity and concision in these pages, does not exist and would have no scientific relevance even if it did.

Science, as al-Haytham could have told these creatures, is not done by mere head count: "The seeker after truth does not put his faith in any consensus, however venerable or widespread. Instead he questions what he has learned of it, applying to it his hard-won scientific knowledge, and he inspects and inquires and investigates and checks and checks and checks again. The road to the truth is long and hard, but that is the road we must follow."

Gregory Wrightstone is a man of true science, firmly in the tradition of al-Haytham. His mission in this book is not to prop up some failed Party Line willy-nilly, nor—on the other hand—unthinkingly to oppose that Party Line merely on the basis that it is as scientifically disagreeable as it is histrionically hysterical. His mission is to distinguish what *is* from what *is not* in the climate debate. He has splendidly succeeded.

It has been a pleasure to play a small part in editing *Inconvenient Facts*. The reader will find the book easy to read, logically structured, clearly expressed, well illustrated, compellingly supported by evidence and, above all, authoritative. This is not an academic work. For one thing, it is written in plain English. Yet it is as comprehensively referenced as any scientific book, and its conclusions are more reliable than those of the small number of "scientific" papers about climate change that the mainstream news media find expedient to mention.

One of the many remarkable things about this book is how startlingly numerous, relevant and compelling are the Inconvenient Facts that it presents, and yet how unbecomingly few of these facts have ever appeared in any mainstream news medium.

The voters cannot be fairly or fully informed where the news media, long captured by hate-filled, totalitarian enemies of the liberty and prosperity of the West and of the democracy that is the guarantor of both, will not fairly or fully report both sides of issues such as the climate question. Their shameful failure is Mr. Wrightstone's shining opportunity. His book is necessary, precisely because the usual news outlets behave as though they were run by the KGB Disinformation Directorate or by Herr Goebbels' *Reichs-propagandaamt*. Whenever the Party Line runs counter to the truth, they do not report the truth at all—except occasionally to mischaracterize it sneeringly as "denialism". Mr. Wrightstone, by contrast, reports the truth whichever way it points, and leaves the reader to make up his own mind.

In the long debate about the influence of Man on climate, the profiteers of doom have sullenly adhered to the Party Line not because it is true (for this book shows beyond reasonable doubt that it is not true) but because, false though the Party Line be, they find it socially convenient, politically expedient and, above all, financially profitable.

One of the two principles of natural justice recognized in the law of the English-speaking countries is *Audiatur et altera pars*— "Let both sides be fairly heard". Given that on this, as on many issues, the news media no longer allow the skeptical side of the case to be heard, well researched, clearly written, beautifully presented and, above all, fact-packed books such as *Inconvenient Facts* are absolutely essential to the very survival of democracy, to the restoration of true science, and to the ultimate triumph of objective truth.

Monckton of Brenchley

Contents

List of Figures

Introduction

Climate Science and the Non-Expert Problem

The whole aim of practical politics is to keep the populace alarmed—and hence clamorous to be led to safety—by menacing it with an endless series of hobgoblins, all of them imaginary.
— H.L. Mencken

You have been exposed to a constant drumbeat from governments, institutions and the media, warning of a looming environmental apocalypse due to human-caused climate change. You have been warned that unless society makes radical changes to our lives, primarily in energy consumption, we will have an increasing number of floods, droughts, hurricanes, tornadoes, heat waves, and inundations of coastlines.

You are told that any climate change is entirely the result of people introducing large amounts of "greenhouse gases" (mostly carbon dioxide) into the atmosphere, and that natural forces have little or no effect on these changes. You have also been told that these assertions are a product of "settled science," agreed upon by 97% of all scientists.

Yet you are not quite buying into this climate doomsday scenario, perhaps because you have seen many situations where "experts" were proven to be completely incorrect, or perhaps because skeptics of the "settled science" make amazingly good sense. You may also realize that models used to predict future temperatures are incredibly complicated, and that those models require human judgement that allows for variables. Finally, you may have noticed that the term *global warming* morphed into *climate change* in the mid-2000s, after the predicted warming stopped, and that *climate change* is now the scapegoat for every weather event considered unusual.

I had many of the same questions concerning the science behind climate-change alarmism. These led me to a deep dive into the methods of the scientists and the validity of what was reported as scientific fact. As a geoscientist who has dealt with various aspects of the Earth's processes for more than 35 years, I know that the brief hundred or so years of recorded temperatures—and the even shorter time frame since the first satellite was launched—is just a blink of a geologic eye. It is too brief a period to evaluate the data adequately. Much of climate science deals with the few decades of recorded data available, and does not attempt to place this data in the longer geologic perspective needed to analyze it adequately.

Scientists who claim that global catastrophe is lurking right around the corner because of the increased production of greenhouse gases sound like they have the facts on their side, but so do the skeptics who dispute them. They both can't be right. Which is it? So, you are questioning the premise of catastrophic climate change, but you are not a scientist, and likely don't believe that you have the necessary skills to evaluate adequately the competing claims.

This is what Scott Adams (the creator of *Dilbert*) calls the non-expert problem. People suspect something is amiss with the one-sided deluge of information about climate catastrophe, but aren't fully equipped to assess it and judge for themselves. This is the purpose of this book: to provide non-scientists with well-documented, easily understood data on the basics of the science, while spotlighting the many glaring flaws in the climate-catastrophe arguments. It is my goal that, armed with the information in this book, you can respond confidently to those advancing misinformation concerning our changing climate.

You will find in these pages many highly significant and, for the climate-catastrophe crowd, *inconvenient facts*. These are facts that the purveyors of impending doom have not publicized for good reason. They reveal that the climate disasters they have prophesied are nothing more than the imaginary hobgoblins about which H. L. Mencken warned us. The inconvenient facts presented here show that the threat to humankind is not climate change or global warming, but a group of men (and women) intent on imposing an agenda based on severely flawed science.

The great tragedy of science, the slaying of a beautiful theory by an ugly fact.

— Thomas Huxley

I. Global Warming — The Basics

1. Greenhouse Gases — Our Security Blanket

The *greenhouse effect*, the important mechanism by which the Earth remains, for the most part, comfortably warm, cozy and livable, is also the pretext for the advancement of doomsday predictions about carbon dioxide-driven global warming. Since this theory is central to climate change debate, and to every chapter in this book, it would be helpful for you to have a basic understanding of the process. As you probably first learned about greenhouse warming in high school science class, the details are most likely lost in the same fog of time that prevents you from remembering how to solve advanced polynomial equations, and what the capital of New Hampshire happens to be. (That's Concord.)

While about 30% of the Sun's radiation is reflected by clouds, most of it passes through the Earth's atmosphere and strikes the surface. There it is absorbed and its energy emitted in the near-infrared spectrum. Some of that re-emitted energy is absorbed by greenhouse-gas molecules. As they absorb the radiation, they in turn emit energy in the form of heat. This is the *greenhouse effect* (Fig. I-1).

Greenhouse gases and the warming they cause keep the Earth at a comfortable average temperature* of about 15° Celsius (59° Fahrenheit). Without them, the Earth would be an unlivable -18°C (-0.4°F). Good examples of the extremes of greenhouse warming are two nearby planets, as they bookend the spectrum of greenhouse gas concentration. Venus has a pea-soup atmosphere, with CO_2 comprising 96% (compared with *0.04%* for Earth), and an average temperature of almost 462°C (863°F). Meanwhile, Mars has virtually *no* atmosphere, and a temperature of -55°C (-67°F). This is the "Goldilocks effect" (Table I-1): Venus is too hot; Mars is too cold; Earth is just right.

---

* *Virtually all climate science deals with temperatures in degrees Celsius. The conversion to Fahrenheit will be made and listed in red where deemed necessary for our American readers.*

Figure I-1: The greenhouse effect

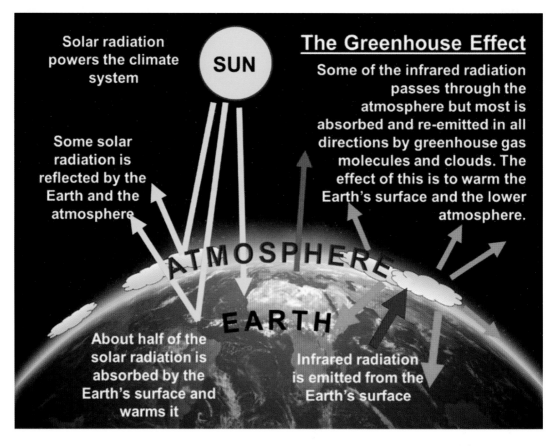

(Modified from IPCC 2007)

Table I-1: The "Goldilocks effect"

Planet	Atmospheric composition	Relative size of greenhouse effect	Mean surface temperature
Venus	96% CO_2	100	462°C (863°F)
Earth	0.04% CO_2: ideal for life	1	15°C (59°F)
Mars	95% CO_2	0.1	-55°C (-67°F)

In the discussion about greenhouse gases, alarmist organizations and their allies in the media focus solely on man-made gases as the main agents of greenhouse warming. They do not mention the most significant greenhouse gas of all—water vapor.

For example, the *National Geographic* climate-change website reports that greenhouse gases "include carbon dioxide (CO_2), methane, nitrous oxide (N_2O), fluorinated gases, and ozone." EPA's greenhouse-gas pie chart is something like the left-hand chart in Fig. I-2. It shows no contribution from water vapor. Based solely on charts like this and descriptions like that given by *National Geographic*, one might well conclude that CO_2 is the main driver of greenhouse warming. The main driver of greenhouse warming—water vapor—is often completely ignored.

Figure I-2: The contribution of greenhouse gases to global warming

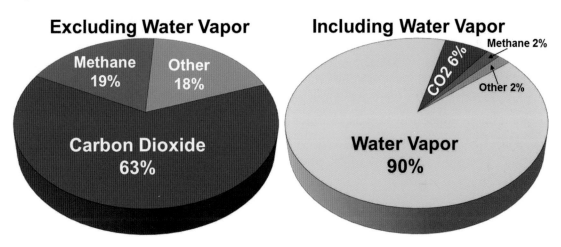

(GHG Data source: CDIAC 2016, water vapor effect: Robinson 2012)

An easily understandable example of the role that water vapor plays in retaining heat comes from the southwest of the United States, where a summer evening walk in the near zero humidity of New Mexico may require a jacket, while your friends in Houston are sweltering in the high heat and humidity and dare not venture out at all.

Both sides of the issue agree that water vapor is responsible for the lion's share of the greenhouse effect, though the percentage of warming attributed has been in dispute. There is no agreement, however, on how much warming will occur due to increases in greenhouse gases, or on how much of that warming has been, or will be, man-made.

Warming allows the atmosphere to increase the amount of water vapor it can carry, which can then add to the greenhouse warming effect (water-vapor feedback), but neither side agrees on the magnitude of this "multiplier" effect on global warming.

Overblown estimates of water-vapor feedback will lead inescapably to overestimation of future warming in the climate models. These overestimates have been identified as one of the main reasons that these models have failed.

Be that as it may, the truth about water vapor is the first *inconvenient fact* in this book.

Inconvenient Fact 1

Carbon dioxide is not the primary greenhouse gas.

Before global warming became a political issue, it was generally accepted among physicists that water vapor contributes 60 to 95% of the greenhouse effect. It is no more sensible or workable for governments to attempt to regulate the weather by declaring CO_2 to be a pollutant than it would be for them to try to regulate water vapor or declare *it* to be a pollutant.

The role of water vapor within climate models and predictions based on it is an inexact science, as the amount of water vapor in the air varies markedly from place to place and from day to day. Absolute humidity can range from near zero in deserts and Antarctica—the Earth's driest continent—to about 4% in the steamy tropics (Driessen 2014). Even a very small change in water vapor, however, can so affect the greenhouse effect as would a doubling of the present CO_2 concentration in the atmosphere (Robinson 2012).

Downplaying or disregarding water vapor, or assigning too large a magnitude to feedbacks such as the water-vapor feedback that is thought to amplify the direct warming from CO_2, serves to overemphasize Man's contribution to greenhouse warming.

Inconvenient Fact 2

The warming effect of CO_2 declines as its concentration increases.

Climate scientists have determined, and both sides agree, that the warming effect of each molecule of CO_2 decreases significantly (logarithmically) as its concentration increases. This is one reason why there was no runaway greenhouse warming when the concentration of CO_2 was approaching 20 times that of today. This inconvenient fact, important though it is, is kept very well hidden and is rarely mentioned, for it undermines the theory of future catastrophic climate change (Hoskins 2014).

Diminishing returns apply (Fig. I-3).

Figure I-3: Less global warming for each additional 50 parts-per-million-by-volume of CO_2 concentration

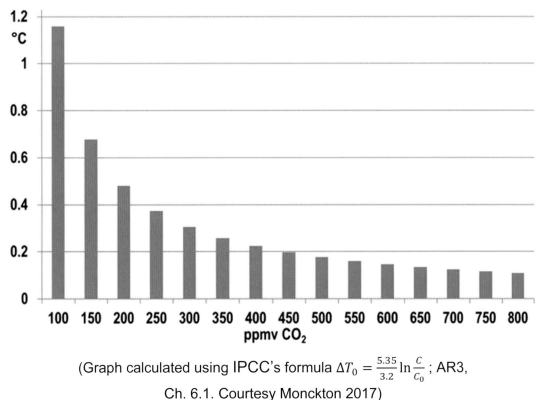

(Graph calculated using IPCC's formula $\Delta T_0 = \frac{5.35}{3.2} \ln \frac{C}{C_0}$; AR3, Ch. 6.1. Courtesy Monckton 2017)

Summary — Greenhouse Gases

There is no dispute among scientists that CO_2 is a greenhouse gas, and that increasing CO_2 concentrations will increase global temperature to some degree. The $100 trillion question is: *To what degree?* The proponents of man-made warming will tell you emphatically that CO_2 is the prime cause of current temperature changes, while, as we shall see in subsequent chapters, true science demonstrates that the slight warming caused by CO_2 is likely largely overwhelmed by the same natural climate drivers that have been active for hundreds of millions of years.

2. Carbon Dioxide — The Foundation of Life, the Food of Plants

Carbon dioxide, or CO_2, is portrayed as the chief villain in the theory of catastrophic global warming. The belief that our carbon-based lifestyles will lead to an environmental Armageddon is fueling a multitude of anti-carbon initiatives, including efforts to stop the use of the three primary, carbon-based sources of energy: coal, oil and natural gas. It has been estimated that the "solutions" to global warming under the Paris agreement would cost the people of the world $100 trillion in lost wealth by 2100. According to Lomborg (2016), that $100 trillion would reduce global temperature by *one-sixth of a degree Celsius* (0.31°F).

In December 2009, the U.S. Environmental Protection Agency (EPA) issued a finding that carbon dioxide would be regulated as a pollutant because it "threatens the public health and welfare of current and future generations." A month before the EPA finding was announced, Barack Obama declared that the U.S. would reduce its emissions of CO_2 by five-sixths of the 2005 levels over the next 30 years. As the Washington pundit George Will noted, a reduction of that size means that per-capita emissions would be about the same as they were in 1875 (Will 2009).

Calculatedly damaging proposals, such as that of the U.N.'s Paris Climate Agreement, are all based on the questionable predictions of more than one hundred complex computer models of the climate. These models predict that a small rise in CO_2 concentration, *altering the atmosphere by just 1 part in 2,000 by the end of this century,* will cause a dramatic and harmful warming of the world's weather (IPCC 2013).

Efforts by environmental activists and government entities to stop pipelines, "keep fossil fuels in the ground," and embrace "renewables," such as solar and wind power, are driven by this unjustifiable aversion to CO_2. The cost to our quality of life is already massive and would worsen as the decades pass if the anti-carbon proposals such as those in the Paris Accord were to be enacted.

The policies proposed to reduce our reliance on carbon dioxide are economically harmful. They also raise several questions critical to the climate debate. (Yes, Virginia, there is a debate.) These questions are addressed in this chapter:

Is today's CO_2 concentration unusually high?
How much of today's CO_2 concentration is man-made?
Would higher CO_2 concentrations be dangerous or beneficial?

The concentration of CO_2 in the air has increased from about 280 parts per million (ppm) by volume in the mid-18th century, to a little above 400 ppm today. If we view the recent CO_2 data through the narrow time-frame of a few decades or centuries, this increase of 120 ppm in CO_2 concentration appears significant. Yet appearances are deceiving.

We shall look first at current and recent CO_2 levels. Then we shall travel back in geological time to get a long-term perspective. This will show clearly that our current levels of CO_2, while rising, are significantly lower than they have been during nearly all of Earth's history. We shall see also that today's low CO_2 concentration is starving trees and plants of the food they need to achieve their full growth potential via photosynthesis.

Inconvenient Fact 3

First and foremost, CO_2 is plant food.

CO_2: The Basics

Nearly 99% of the atmosphere consists of nitrogen and oxygen. The remaining 1% consists of several trace gases (Fig. I-4), including CO_2, whose current concentration represents just 0.04% of the atmosphere, or 400 molecules out of every million. Current levels are an incredibly small percentage of the atmosphere, albeit an important one, as advanced plant life could not survive without at least 150 ppm. As we shall see, that 150 ppm "line of death" is dangerously close to recent concentrations.

Figure I-4: Gases in the atmosphere, excluding water vapor

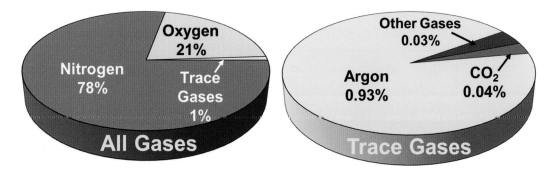

(Source data from U.S. National Weather Service)

The largest contributor to CO_2 from human activities is the burning of fossil fuels for transport, heating, cooking, power, and a myriad of other uses. Using these fuels, we enjoy our modern conveniences, make our livings and enjoy healthier and longer lives than anybody in all of history (Fig. I-5).

Figure I-5: Sources of man-made CO_2 emissions

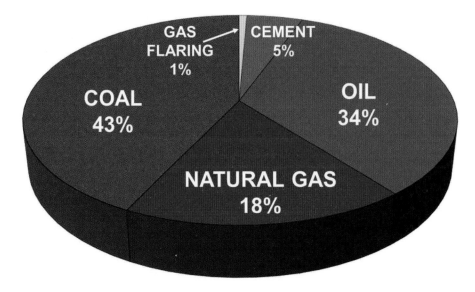

(Source data: Le Quéré 2012)

Interestingly, cleaner-burning, lower-cost, natural gas has been increasing its share of the energy sector. It emits significantly less CO_2 per unit of thermal energy than either coal or gasoline (Fig. I-6).

Figure I-6: Pounds of CO_2 emitted, per million British Thermal Units
(BTU, i.e., energy output)

Fuel	Pounds CO_2/million BTUs
Coal (bituminous)	206
Gasoline	157
Natural gas	117

(Source data: US EIA 2017)

Recent global CO_2 emissions have been dominated by China, the United States, the European Union and India (Boden 2017). These four were responsible for 61% of worldwide CO_2, with about 190 countries making up the rest (Fig. I-7).

Figure I-7: CO_2 emissions by country, 2014

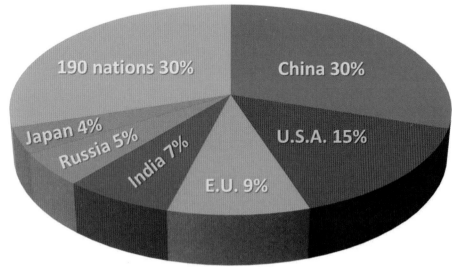

(Source data: Boden 2017)

Earth's Carbon Dioxide History

Direct atmospheric CO_2 measurements began in 1958 at the Mauna Loa Observatory, Hawaii. They show a steady rise in CO_2 from 314 ppm in 1958 to 406 ppm in early 2017 (Fig. I-8).

The 40% increase, from 280 ppm in 1750 to 406 ppm in 2017, is widely recognized to be mainly man-made. This would be primarily from energy consumption, but also from cement manufacture, and a small amount from the flaring of natural gas. A longer-term view (Fig. I-9) shows global CO_2 emissions began rising very slightly in the mid-1850s, with a significant acceleration since the mid-20th Century.

Is today's CO_2 concentration of ~400 ppm unprecedented, unusual, or in any way dangerous? What happened in the early climate, when CO_2 concentrations very much higher than today's prevailed?

Figure I-8: Mauna Loa CO_2 concentration, 1958 – 2017

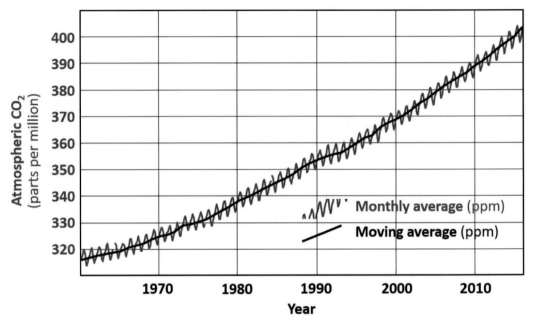

(Source data: Tans 2017)

Figure I-9: Global man-made CO_2 emissions

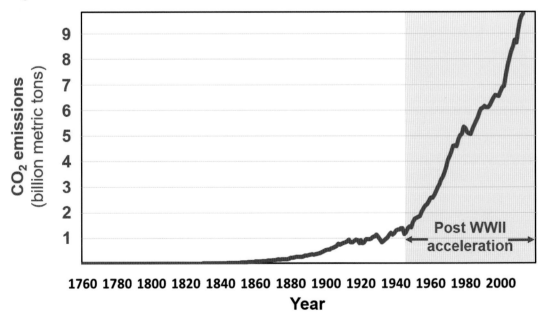

(Source data: Boden 2016)

Fortunately for researchers of historic CO_2 levels, accurate reconstructions of atmospheric CO_2 concentrations are available for hundreds of thousands of years from ice cores taken from Antarctica and Greenland. Air bubbles trapped within the layers of snowfall that compacted to form the glacial ice allow accurate dating and direct measurement of the ancient gases.

Antarctica has had the longest continuous accumulations of ice. It provides data going back 800,000 years, while data from Greenland provides very useful information on Northern Hemisphere concentrations dating back to the previous interglacial period, 128,000 years ago.

Fig. I-10 shows a 100,000-year record from Antarctica, dating back to the beginning of the most recent ice age. This shows the typical CO_2 concentration decline during the glacial period, and the rise during the warmer interglacial period. We see that there was a rise of about 120 ppm since pre-industrial times. Is this just a normal increase during an interglacial period, or is it abnormally high?

Figure I-10: 100,000 years of CO_2 data from the Vostok ice core, Antarctica

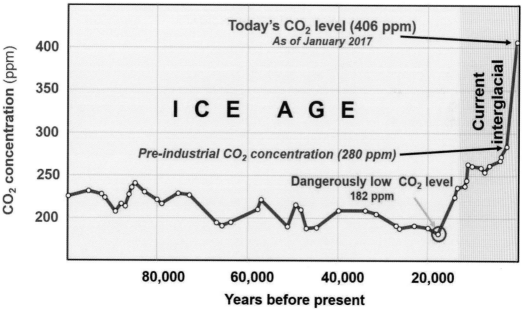

(Source data: Barnola 2003)

Going further back, we see CO_2 levels averaged about 280 ppm during similar stages of each of the interglacial periods (Fig. I-11). The current level of 400 ppm is higher by about 120 ppm, or ~40% higher than the standard for preceding warm periods.

Figure I-11: 400,000 years of CO_2 data from the Vostok ice core, Antarctica

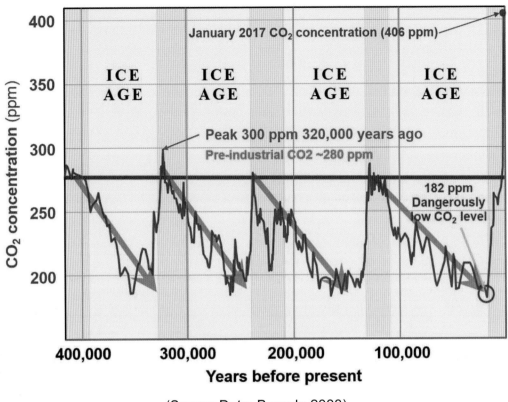

(Source Data: Barnola 2003)

Inconvenient Fact 4

In the last four ice ages, the CO_2 level was dangerously low.

During each of the last four ice ages, CO_2 concentration fell below 190 ppm. At the end of the last ice age, it fell to 182 ppm, thought to be the lowest in the Earth's history. Why is this alarming? Because below 150 ppm, most terrestrial plant life cannot exist. We came within about 30 ppm (30 molecules out of every one million) to the extinction of most plant life on land, and with it the extinction of all higher terrestrial life-forms that depend on it. Bear in mind that, before we began adding CO_2 to the atmosphere, we weren't sure that we wouldn't cross that critical 150-ppm threshold during the next glacial period. (That period may be coming sooner than we think.)

Both the relatively short-term data from ice cores shown above in Figure I-11, and much longer-term data going back 140 million years (Berner 2001, Fig. I-12) show an alarming downward trend toward CO_2 starvation. The combustion of fossil fuels has allowed humanity to increase concentrations of this beneficial molecule, and perhaps avert an actual CO_2-related climate apocalypse.

Inconvenient Fact 5

140-million-year trend of dangerously decreasing CO_2

Figure I-12: The dangerous 140-million-year decline in CO_2

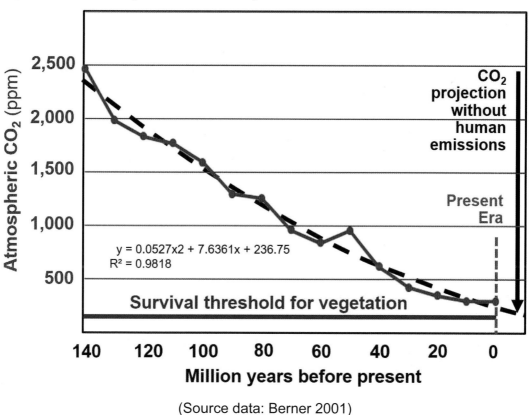

(Source data: Berner 2001)

The forecasters of climate doom say—correctly, as far as it goes—that the CO_2 level has never been this high in at least the last 400,000 years. They prefer to view the increase of about 120 ppm over the last 150 years through the narrow lens of recent geological time. To properly analyze the current levels, we need to jump into our "Way Back Machine." When we put the data into the proper context, it leads us to our next inconvenient fact.

Inconvenient Fact 6

Our current geologic period (Quaternary) has the lowest average CO₂ levels in the history of the Earth.

Contrary to the oft-repeated mantra of the media and the so-called "experts" that today's CO_2 concentration is unprecedented, our current geologic period, the Quaternary, has seen the lowest average levels of carbon dioxide in the Earth's long history. Though CO_2 concentrations briefly peaked 320,000 years ago at 300 ppm, the average for the past 800,000 years was 230 ppm (Luthi 2008).

The average CO_2 concentration in the preceding 600 million years (Fig. I-13) was more than 2,600 ppm, nearly seven times our current amount and *2.5 times the worst case predicted by the IPCC for 2100*. Our current geologic period (Quaternary) has the *lowest average CO₂ concentration* in the history of the Earth (Fig. I-14).

Figure I-13: Carbon Dioxide—600 Million Years of Data

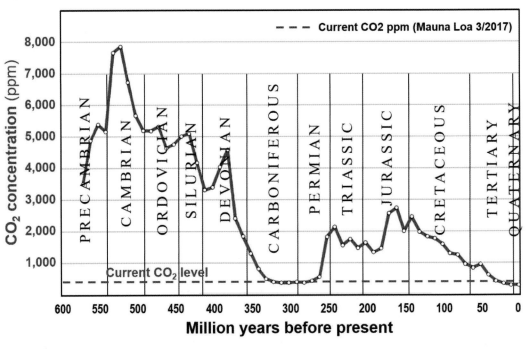

(Source data: Berner 2001)

It should be obvious to impartial observers of the long-term data that, rather than experiencing excessively high levels of carbon dioxide, we are in fact in a period of CO_2 starvation. While short historical periods are used to support apocalyptic visions of life in a world with slightly increased CO_2, perspective is everything: the increase of ~120 ppm since the beginning of the Industrial Revolution is barely recognizable when viewed in the context of a longer section of Earth's CO_2 history.

Figure I-14: Average CO_2 concentrations in 11 geological periods

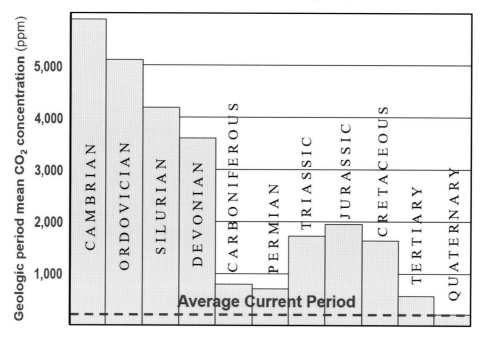

(Source data: Berner 2001)

Is 400 PPM Really a CO_2 Tipping Point?

We are on the precipice of climate system tipping points beyond which there is no redemption.

— James Hansen, Former head of NASA's Goddard Institute for Space Studies

This March [2014], global levels of CO_2 passed 400 ppm ... Already we are seeing the deadly effects of climate change in the form of rising seas, monster storms, wildfires, and extreme weather of all kinds. Passing 400 ppm is an ominous sign of what might come next.

— 350.org

The notion of a "tipping point" is not science. It is propaganda. The climate extremists have declared, on no evidence, that 400 ppm CO_2 is a "tipping point" beyond which the Earth cannot recover, without a drastic reduction in CO_2 emission. Never mind that, as Fig. I-13 shows, CO_2 levels were many multiples of 400 ppm during virtually all of Earth's history. This "tipping point" was an entirely arbitrary round number selected because it would soon be reached. The "tipping point" might just as easily—and just as arbitrarily—have been set at 425 ppm, but that would have delayed the supposed launch of climate Armageddon to 2020 or later. It would have diminished the Damoclean fear of impending doom needed to pass the economically destructive anti-CO_2 legislation that would damage the West and the world.

The Social Benefits of Increasing Carbon

It has been well documented that more CO_2 directly benefits plant growth. De Saussure (1804) was the first to link high CO_2 concentration to faster plant growth. Since then, many thousands of peer-reviewed studies have backed up his conclusion. Research has also shown that increased CO_2 helps plants to resist drought, warmer weather, pollution and other environmental stresses.

Inconvenient Fact 7

More CO_2 means more plant growth.

Inconvenient Fact 8

More CO_2 helps to feed more people worldwide.

In the "Biological Change" section of the Nongovernmental International Panel on Climate Change (NIPCC) *Climate Change Reconsidered* (Idso 2014), the benefits of higher CO_2 concentration to the production of the world's food are listed. Here are the main points:

Nearly all plants increase photosynthesis in response to increasing CO_2 ("CO_2 fertilization").

More CO_2 makes plants grow faster, and with less stress and less water.

Forests are growing faster in response to increasing CO_2.

More CO_2 stimulates growth of beneficial bacteria in both soil and water.

CO_2 fertilization, leading to more plant growth, means less erosion of topsoil.

More CO_2 means bigger crop yields, and more and bigger flowers.

More CO_2 fosters glomalin, a beneficial protein created by root fungi.

More CO_2 means less water loss, less irrigation, and more soil moisture.

More CO_2 helps plants to create natural repellants to fight insect predators.

A summary of 270 laboratory studies (Idso, 2013) of 83 food crops showed that increasing CO_2 concentrations by 300 ppm will increase plant growth by an average of 46% across all crops studied (dry-weight biomass). Fig. I-15 shows 45 crops, with the percentage increase expected from each crop, and (color-coded) with the cash benefit to the global economy resulting from the CO_2-driven increase in crop yield for that crop in the half-century from 1961 to 2010.

Conversely, a large number of studies show the adverse effects of a low-CO_2 environment. For instance, Overdieck (1988) indicated that, compared to today, plant growth was reduced by 8% in the period before the Industrial Revolution, with its low concentration of 280 ppm CO_2.

While it is only common sense that plants thrive in response to higher CO_2 concentrations, it is also relevant that the ancestors of the plants on which we rely first evolved and prospered when CO_2 levels were *up to 10 times today's levels*. Therefore, the proposed attempts by climate extremists to reduce CO_2 concentrations would be bad for plants, bad for animals, and bad for humankind.

Although I do not pretend to speak for the planet's flora, I am quite certain that, if plants had a say in the matter, they would not be lobbying for reductions in CO_2 levels. For plants, CO_2 is food. They need more of it, not less.

Inconvenient Fact 9

More CO_2 means moister soil.

Figure I-15: Crop yield growth and cash benefit with 300 ppm more CO_2
(based on 3,586 experiments on 549 plant species)

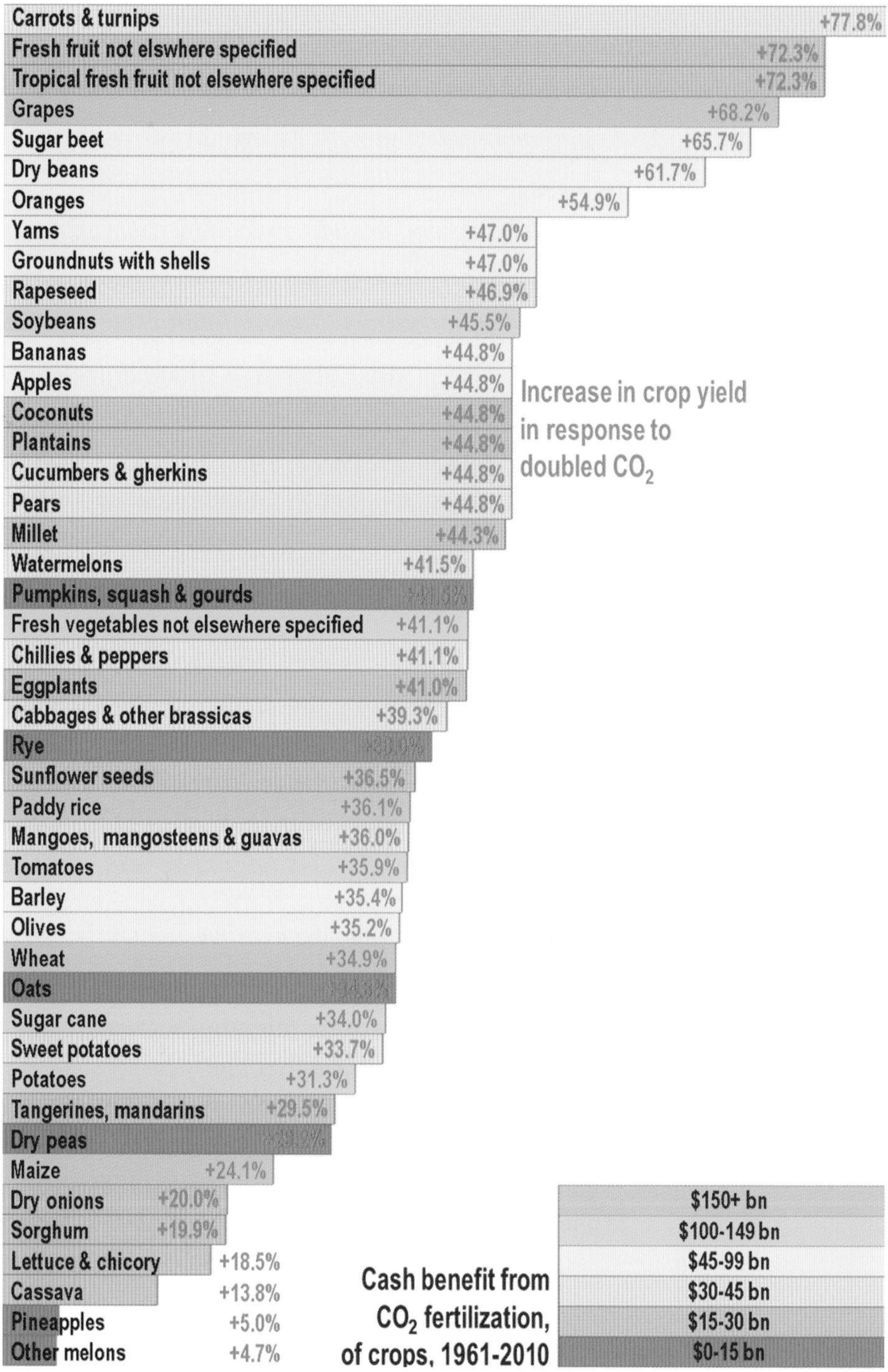

Crop	Increase
Carrots & turnips	+77.8%
Fresh fruit not elswhere specified	+72.3%
Tropical fresh fruit not elsewhere specified	+72.3%
Grapes	+68.2%
Sugar beet	+65.7%
Dry beans	+61.7%
Oranges	+54.9%
Yams	+47.0%
Groundnuts with shells	+47.0%
Rapeseed	+46.9%
Soybeans	+45.5%
Bananas	+44.8%
Apples	+44.8%
Coconuts	+44.8%
Plantains	+44.8%
Cucumbers & gherkins	+44.8%
Pears	+44.8%
Millet	+44.3%
Watermelons	+41.5%
Pumpkins, squash & gourds	+41.5%
Fresh vegetables not elsewhere specified	+41.1%
Chillies & peppers	+41.1%
Eggplants	+41.0%
Cabbages & other brassicas	+39.3%
Rye	+38.5%
Sunflower seeds	+36.5%
Paddy rice	+36.1%
Mangoes, mangosteens & guavas	+36.0%
Tomatoes	+35.9%
Barley	+35.4%
Olives	+35.2%
Wheat	+34.9%
Oats	+34.8%
Sugar cane	+34.0%
Sweet potatoes	+33.7%
Potatoes	+31.3%
Tangerines, mandarins	+29.5%
Dry peas	+29.3%
Maize	+24.1%
Dry onions	+20.0%
Sorghum	+19.9%
Lettuce & chicory	+18.5%
Cassava	+13.8%
Pineapples	+5.0%
Other melons	+4.7%

Increase in crop yield in response to doubled CO_2

Cash benefit from CO_2 fertilization, of crops, 1961-2010

$150+ bn
$100-149 bn
$45-99 bn
$30-45 bn
$15-30 bn
$0-15 bn

(Idso 2013, courtesy Monckton 2017)

There is a growing realization that more CO_2 in the air means more moisture in the soil, as Swann reveals (2016). The major cause of water loss in plants is attributable to transpiration, in which the stomata or pores on the undersides of the leaves are open to absorb CO_2. With more CO_2, the stomata are open for shorter periods, the leaves lose less water, and more moisture remains in the soil.

These benefits are extremely important to our future ability to feed a growing population, as observed by Madhu (2015). He reports on the beneficial results of increasing CO_2 on soybean growth:

> *These results show a direct and interactive effect of elevated [CO₂] and soil moisture on plant growth that will affect not only ... global food security but also nutritional security.*

We will look at the benefits of CO_2 in more detail later, when we deal with the various imaginary climate apocalypses. For now, let us note that decreases in drought, heat waves and forest fires have all been linked to CO_2-related increases in soil moisture. Benefits such as these from increased CO_2 concentration are inconvenient facts that the climate extremists would prefer to suppress. They are seldom included in official economic assessments of the supposed "social cost" of climate change.

Summary — CO₂ and Humankind

Rather than being at unprecedentedly high levels, CO_2 is at one of its lowest concentrations in the long history of the Earth. What has been called a miracle molecule, CO_2 in greater amounts is greening the Earth with an astonishing increase in the productivity of plants and trees worldwide—an increase so dramatic that it can been seen by satellites from space. As usual, this good news is just the opposite of what we are being told by those who call themselves "green."

The attempt to demonize CO_2 as dangerously high at more than 400 ppm is nothing more than another of H. L. Mencken's hobgoblins of alarm. It is conveniently calculated to cause fear, so that people will docilely accept drastic and economically destructive policies. So far, the global-warming hobgoblin has been extraordinarily effective. Most governments now have in place economically damaging regimes of taxation and regulation intended to curtail the use of fossil fuels. The policies themselves are scientifically baseless and economically senseless, and their cost, in lives and treasure, is heavy.

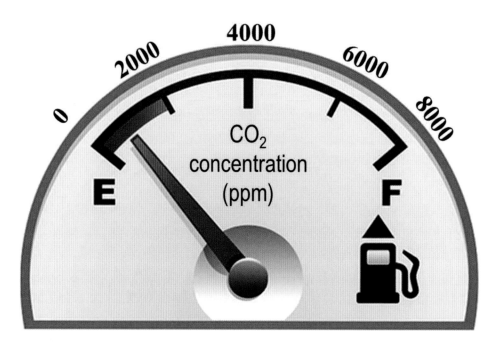

Worrying that 400 ppm is too high is like worrying about your fuel tank overflowing when it reaches the 1/8 mark during filling.
— Pierre Gosselin

What historians will definitely wonder about in future centuries is how deeply flawed logic, obscured by shrewd and unrelenting propaganda, actually enabled a coalition of powerful special interests to convince nearly everyone in the world that carbon dioxide from human industry was a dangerous, planet-destroying toxin.

   It will be remembered as the greatest mass delusion in the history of the world—that carbon dioxide, the life of plants, was considered for a time to be a deadly poison.
— Ed Ring 2008

3. Temperature — A Question of Degree

We saw in the last chapter how proponents of man-made climate hysteria have mischaracterized current and predicted concentrations of carbon dioxide. CO_2 is demonized because of the supposed link between it, warmer weather and a host of purported catastrophes.

As with *carbon dioxide*, most of the media-driven hysteria and climate-science research on *temperature* has focused on the recent record: just 250 years for thermometers and the past 50 years for satellites. And, as with CO_2 reporting, a focus only on these relatively short time spans tends to provide a skewed interpretation of the data.

For example, the climate alarmists tell us that the warming of recent decades is unusual and unprecedented. They also breathlessly report that last month or year or decade (take your pick) was the highest in recorded history. Yet recorded history is a blink of an eye in geological time. The catastrophists are viewing the climate through the narrowly focused lens of modern history. To put the data in its proper context, one needs to take a long-term geologic perspective—thousands and millions of years.

As with CO_2, we will look first at temperatures in the modern era and then place the data in its proper perspective by gradually going back from decades to hundreds of millions of years.

First, however, we must deal with the elephant in the room—perhaps the most pivotal and controversial issue involved in the climate-science debate.

The Hockey-Stick Graph and 'Unprecedented' Global Warming

Until 1998 the "consensus" view was that over the last several thousand years temperatures had risen and fallen as shown in noted climatologist Hubert Lamb's graph (Fig. I-16), reproduced in 1990 in the *First Assessment Report* of the Intergovernmental Panel on Climate Change (IPCC). The graph shows warming beginning in the late-17th century as the Earth began to come out of the coldest portion of the Little Ice Age (1250 – 1850), followed by recent temperatures significantly less than those experienced in the Medieval Warm Period (950 – 1250).

This view, which prevailed before the politicization of climate science, was based on extensive historical documents and measured temperatures. It was understood that several previous warm periods had occurred over the last 10,000 years (including the Modern, Medieval, Roman, Minoan, Egyptian Old-Kingdom and Holocene climate optima) and that *all were warmer than today,* even though CO_2

concentration was only 70% of today's. This inconvenient contradiction of lower CO_2 and higher temperatures did not fit the template that connected rising CO_2 to a harmful temperature increase to justify draconian measures for reducing our carbon footprint.

Even more inconvenient was that our current warming trend had *actually begun more than 200 years before any significant man-made contribution to the greenhouse gases in the atmosphere.* The traditional scientific account of the recent history of our planet's temperature could not be allowed to stand if the theory of catastrophic human-induced warming were to be accepted.

Figure I-16: Hubert Lamb's temperature graph of the past 1,100 years

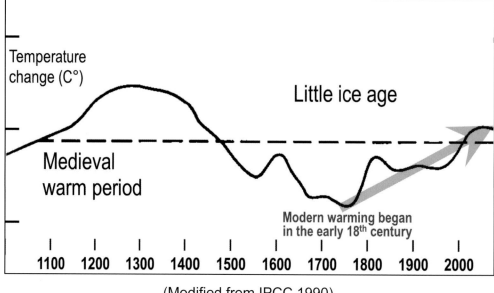

(Modified from IPCC 1990)

Enter Michael Mann, a hitherto unknown climate scientist. Mann, with two colleagues, published two papers (Mann 1998 and 1999) that purported to reconstruct 1,000 years of the Earth's temperature. They stated that "temperatures in the latter half of the 20th century were unprecedented" and that "even the warmer intervals in the reconstruction pale in comparison with mid-to-late 20th-century temperatures."

Their results were summarized in a graph that has become a poster child for claims of human-driven temperature increases (Fig. I-17). It featured steadily declining temperatures from 1000 – 1900 A.D., followed by rapidly increasing temperatures in the 20th century. The well-documented Medieval Warm Period was suddenly gone, along with the uncomfortably cold Little Ice Age. Most importantly, the sudden ramp up of temperatures coincided with the beginning of the Industrial Revolution and steadily increasing CO_2 levels. Because the graph had a 900-year shaft of slowly declining temperature and then a short blade of rapidly increasing temperature, it was dubbed the "Hockey Stick."

The planet's self-proclaimed climate guardians quickly latched upon the hockey-stick graph as "proof" of a causal link between greenhouse gas and dangerous warming. The graph was a centerpiece of IPCC's *Third Assessment Report* in 2001.

Figure I-17: The Mann-made hockey stick

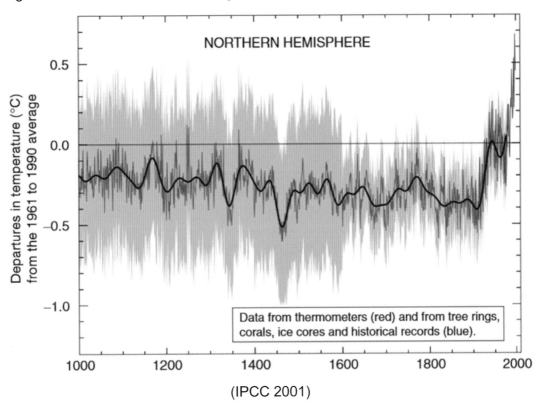

(IPCC 2001)

Why the 'Hockey-Stick' Graph Matters

If Mann's depiction of temperature over the last millennium were correct, then his work might form a solid basis for recent warming being mostly man-made. This infamous chart featured prominently in Al Gore's movie and book *An Inconvenient Truth,* and also as a backdrop to many IPCC press conferences.

Mann's basis for the graph in Fig. I-17 has been heavily criticized. Those who challenged it *include many scientists who support the idea of man-made warming.*

First, Mann relied heavily for temperature proxies on a relatively small dataset of tree-ring data primarily from California bristlecone pines, and a very small sample from cedars on the Gaspé Peninsula (wherever that is).

The IPCC itself had previously issued warnings that tree-ring data are a poor source for temperature reconstruction. The reason is that the width of the annual tree-ring will grow thicker not only when the weather is warmer, but also when it is wetter, or when more CO_2 in the air fertilizes the tree and boosts its growth.

Even the scientists who provided the data for the bristlecone-pine series gave specific warnings against using it for temperature reconstruction. Mann used the data anyway. It provided the results he wanted. Not only did he use questionable proxies, he cherry-picked a relatively small number of tree-rings and ignored a greater number of trees from the same area that did not show the results that he desired.

Secondly, a detailed review by two Canadian researchers (McIntyre 1998) of the mathematical and statistical methodology used by Mann revealed multiple serious errors. Amazingly, no matter what data the two scientists plugged into Mann's formula, it invariably produced a "hockey stick". They concluded, therefore, that Mann's hockey-stick reconstruction of changes in the Earth's temperature was "primarily an artefact (sic) of poor data handling, obsolete data and incorrect calculation of principal components."

> *Absence of the medieval warming in the Hockey Stick graph might simply mean tree ring proxies are unreliable, not that the climate really was relatively cooler.*
> — Professor John Christy, Director of the Earth System Science Center at Univ. of Alabama, Huntsville in testimony to Congress, March 31, 2001 (Steyn 2015)

> *Mann's hockey stick has indeed been substantially discredited*
> — Dr. Hamish Campbell, PhD, Geologist New Zealand's Institute of Geological and Nuclear Sciences

> *We now know that the hockey stick is fraudulent*
> — Dr. Michael R. Fox, Professor of Chemistry at Idaho State University (Steyn 2015)

In the coming sections, we shall see what the actual physical data and historical records really tell us about temperature and about whether our current temperatures are really unusual and unprecedented, as proponents of climate alarmism such as Michael Mann would have us believe. Look at the data. Make up your own mind.

Modern Instrumental Data

There are three ways to measure atmospheric temperature directly using instruments. Each has limitations.

Method	First Used
Land and ocean surface thermometers	1659
Weather balloons	Mid-1950s
Satellites	1979

Satellites are the most reliable temperature measuring tool and have nearly global coverage, but have a very short history. Weather balloons are also reliable but can usually be used only over land and only go back 60 years or so. Thermometers have the longest record: the Central England Temperature Record, dating from 1659, was the first-ever regional record, but their accuracy is somewhat limited because local effects such as increasing urbanization can produce artificial localized warming.

Satellite data for temperature history is preferable to other methods due to the accuracy it provides, but satellites have been providing data for less than 40 years. The data reveals a nearly 20-year trend of warming (1979 – 1998) beginning when the first climate satellites were launched in 1979 (Fig. I-18). That warming trend ended with an exceptionally warm 1998 and then 18 years of essentially flat temperatures.

Figure I-18 Satellite measured global warming since 1979: <0.5°C (0.9°F)

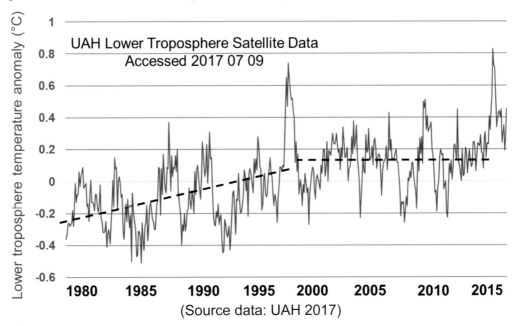

(Source data: UAH 2017)

Using only this satellite data is a bit iffy because of the short temperature history. Additionally, the Earth was just exiting a 33 year-long cooling trend just as the first climate satellite was launched. Because of the long cooling trend, the earliest satellite data likely captured temperatures that were the coldest since the mid-1940s. At the Earth's surface, the two longest-standing terrestrial thermometer datasets are kept up by the U.K. Met Office. They include the HadCRUT4 dataset, which has been continuously updated since 1850, and the Central England temperature record, the world's longest regional record that dates to 1659.

The Intergovernmental Panel on Climate Change (IPCC), and most other agencies promoting a link between human activities and the current warming, use the HadCRUT4 data (Fig. I-19). The graph shows temperature data from 1850 to 2017 derived from direct thermometer readings and reveals that there has been a general overall warming trend of about 0.85°C (1.5°F) over the last 167 years. Significantly, the data collection began around the time that many researchers deem to be near the end of the 500-plus-year "Little Ice Age" in the mid-1850s (more on that later).

Figure I-19: Thermometer data show a temperature increase of 0.85°C
(1.5°F) 1850 – 2017.

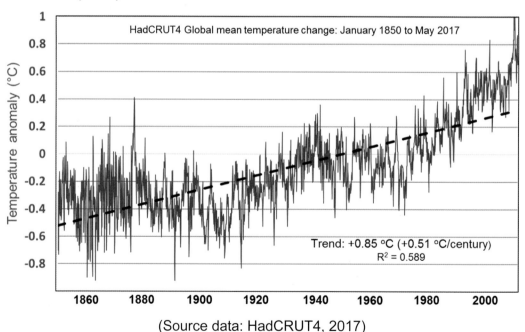

(Source data: HadCRUT4, 2017)

The warming has occurred in fits and starts with three distinct periods of cooling or flat temperatures and two periods of warming. A third period of warming may be occurring now, but time will tell.

The reason that the IPCC and other pro-alarmist groups use the relatively short HadCRUT4 dataset rather than the much longer records that are available is that it is much easier to allege a causal linkage between CO_2 increase and warming if only looking at the relatively short term. If we review the above data and add the human CO_2 emissions, one could make a reasoned argument that there is likely a connection between increasing CO_2 emissions and rising temperature (Fig. I-20). As we have seen in the carbon dioxide section, however, context is everything.

Figure I-20: Temperature vs. CO_2 (1850 – 2013)

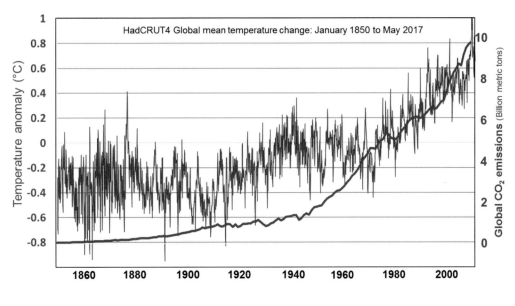

(Source data: Temperature: HadCRUT4, CO_2: Boden 2016)

Two hugely inconvenient facts emerge upon close inspection of the above chart. Significant carbon dioxide emissions didn't start ramping up until shortly after the end of the Second World War. Yet, since 1945, more than 70% of that time frame included periods of either declining or flat temperatures (Fig. I-21).

During two long periods of time from 1945 to 1979 and from 1998 to 2015, temperatures either ceased increasing or actually fell. Both of these long periods coincided with rising CO_2. If CO_2 is driving dangerous warming, as the promoters of anthropogenic global warming (AGW) would have us believe, why did more than 70% of the postwar period show stable or even falling temperatures despite the fact that CO_2 concentrations were inexorably rising? This fact alone should cause any open-minded observer to question the validity of the claims made by those promoting the myth of a radical and dangerous man-made CO_2-driven warming.

Figure I-21: Stable or falling temperatures prevailed in most of the period 1945 – 2016.

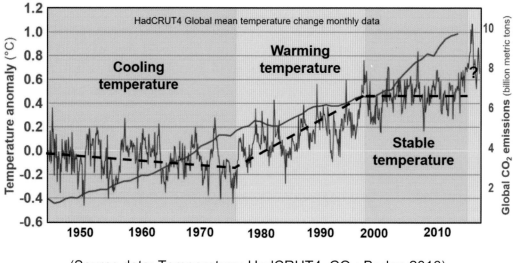

(Source data: Temperature: HadCRUT4, CO_2: Boden 2016)

For nearly 18 years, beginning in 1998, the warming stopped. According to the HadCRUT4 dataset (Fig. I-22) and backed up by satellite and balloon data, the global warming that began in 1976 suddenly and inexplicably stopped. According to global warming theory, humankind's ongoing contribution of CO_2 should have continued to warm the planet's atmosphere. Yet, for almost 18 years, the warming stopped as CO_2 relentlessly increased.

Inconvenient Fact 10

Recent Inconvenient Pause of 18 years in warming, despite rise in CO_2

Realization among the leaders of climate alarm that their supposedly infallible theory had suspended its functioning for some unknown reason forced them to modify their terminology. It was during this long period without warming that *"global warming"* morphed into the all-inclusive term *"climate change."* Now, anything at all out of the ordinary can be attributed to man's climate influences, even though climate, like baseball, sets out-of-the-ordinary records all the time. In the climate, out of the ordinary is ordinary.

Based on the most recent data and confirmed by examination of satellite data, the Inconvenient Pause may have ended in 2015. As we shall see by looking at longer-term data, additional warming probably will continue for at least a portion of this century, but likely not to the levels predicted by the IPCC.

Figure I-22: An inconvenient pause: 18 years of no warming yet CO_2 increased

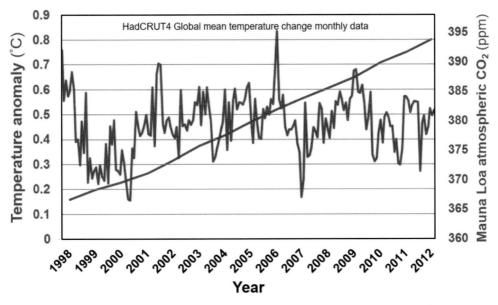

(Source data: Temperature: HadCRUT4, CO_2: Tans 2017)

It's tough to make predictions, especially about the future.
— Yogi Berra

If you can't explain the pause, you can't explain the cause.
— The Hockey Schtick

Much attention has been paid to the recent nearly 18-year Inconvenient Pause in warming shown above in Figure I-22 and rightly so. It is very recent and seems to contradict the main thrust of the alarmists' projections. Just as important as the Pause, but not so much discussed, is the significant 33-year span of global cooling from 1944 – 1976 that coincided with steeply increasing CO_2 concentration as global industrial activity picked up after the Second World War (Fig. I-23).

While studying geology in the 1970s, I was taught that we likely were heading toward another ice age based on the previous 30-plus years of cooling and the fact that our inter-glacial period had persisted for longer than some previous warm periods. This was considered "settled science." It was not a question of *whether* the next ice age would come, but *when*.

Inconvenient Fact 11

CO_2 rose after the Second World War, but temperature fell.

Figure I-23: For 33 postwar years, CO₂ rose quickly but temperature fell.

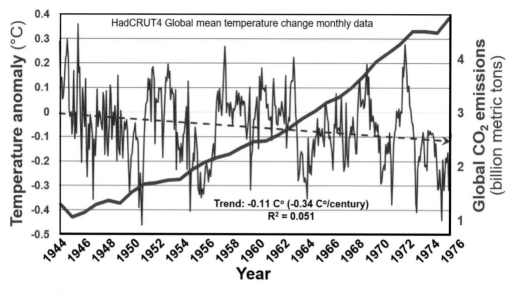

(Source data: Temperature: HadCRUT4 2017, CO₂: Boden 2016)

The facts have emerged, in recent years and months, from research into past ice ages. They imply that the threat of a new ice age must now stand alongside nuclear war as a likely source of wholesale death and misery for mankind.

— Nigel Calder, 1975

If present trends continue, the world will be... eleven degrees colder by the year 2000. This is about twice what it would take us to put us in another ice age.

— Kenneth Watt, during the first Earth Day celebration in 1970

Today's global-warming advocates are as adamant about their beliefs as were yesterday's global-cooling enthusiasts, but they will probably turn out to be just as wrong.

REALLY Inconvenient Fact 12

Modern warming began long before SUVs or coal-fired plants.

As we saw in the last section on carbon dioxide, in the climate debate, context is everything.

Earlier I wrote that, if Michael Mann's modeling of global temperatures were correct, and we had 900 years of cooling followed by a sharp increase in the 20th

Century, then that would be strong evidence linking man's activities to modern warming. The counter-evidence to the Mann argument would be data showing that modern warming began *before* CO_2 began to rise sharply. It would suggest that natural forces were the primary driver of warming prior to 1900 and likely remain so today.

Some Important Charts

The following charts may be some of the most important in the entire book.

These charts demonstrate conclusively that the current trend of increasing temperatures began long before anyone drove the first Model T to the grocery store, and long before CO_2 levels cracked 300 ppm. Multiple lines of evidence support the notion that warming following the Little Ice Age *predated the recent rise in CO_2 concentration.* This inconvenient data is part of the cumulative evidence that will eventually drive the final nails into the coffin of the catastrophic man-made warming theory.

The Central England temperature record (HadCET) contains the longest continuously measured regional temperature dataset in the world, going back more than 350 years. As we shall see, promotion of this longer record by the IPCC would have cut the legs out from under their primary mission of linking human-caused greenhouse gases to harmful increases in temperature. It would also have thoroughly discredited the Mann-made hockey-stick interpretation of steadily lowering temperatures until the 20th century and then a sudden CO_2-driven warming.

The Central England record (Fig. I-24) began in 1659, during some of the coldest temperatures in the last 4,500 years. Its earliest data was captured during a period of extreme cold from 1670 to 1715 that is known as the Maunder Minimum, after Edward Maunder, a researcher at the Royal Observatory at Greenwich, London, who noticed that it coincided with a period of sharp decline in solar activity. The Maunder Minimum was the coldest period during the 600-year Little Ice Age (1250 – 1850), which brought famine, poor harvests, disease and widespread loss of life.

As we shall see, humanity has historically suffered greatly during cold periods. The Little Ice Age was no exception, so the gradual warming that began in the late 1600s was welcome relief to the inhabitants of that period.

The population of northern Europe, who had suffered the most during the Little Ice Age (Iceland, for instance, lost half its population), could not realize it at the time, but the beneficial warming that began in the late 17th century would be used 300 years later by climate alarmists to assert that dangerous man-made greenhouse gases were increasing temperature.

Figure I-24: Greater than 300 years of warming in central England
        from 1695 – 2017

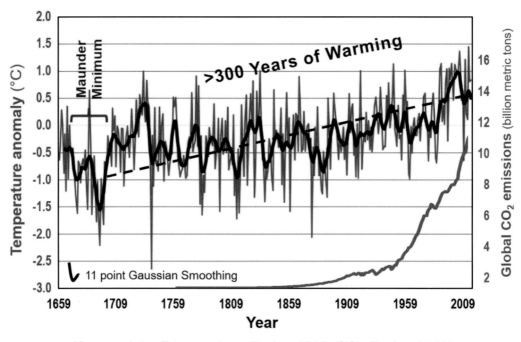

(Source data: Temperature: Parker 1992; CO_2: Boden 2016)

Modern warming that began at the turn of the 18th century continues to this day, more than 300 years later. This gradual recovery from the death-dealing cold of the Little Ice Age was appropriately dubbed "The long, slow thaw" by Tony Brown (2011).

The warming began more than 200 years before any significant contribution of man-made CO_2 to the atmosphere. This early warming was entirely naturally driven and is directly at odds with Mann's hockey-stick depiction of steady cooling during this time. Those natural forces driving the temperature increases in the 18th and 19th centuries did not suddenly cease to act at the dawn of the 20th century.

Inconvenient Fact 13

Melting glaciers and rising seas confirm warming predated increases of CO_2.

Melting glaciers and rising sea levels are the direct result of warming. Supporters of catastrophic human-induced warming often cite them as proof that the weather is warming. Inconveniently for them, however, the evidence shows that the global warming causing the rise in sea levels and the retreat of the glaciers began long before any significant man-made CO_2 increases could have influenced either. Both are directly the result of the natural warming that began in the year 1695.

In about 1250, temperature began its descent into the depths of the Little Ice Age, and in only a couple of decades the waves of cold started the march of the glaciers in both hemispheres (Grove 2001). The advancing ice often had severe consequences for local populations, destroying many villages. The area of Chamonix in southeastern France, for example, is estimated to have lost one-third of its tillable land to avalanches, snow and glaciers (Fagan 2000).

Because these events had profound negative effects on the local populace, detailed records of glacial advances and retreats began to be kept. These records allow us to determine the extent of glaciers with great accuracy going back several hundred years. Figure I-25 shows a summary of glacial-length records from 169 sites around the world relative to their extent in 1950 (Oerlemans 2005).

We saw that the current warming trend began in the late 17th century (Figure I-24), but the glaciers could not begin to retreat until the atmosphere had warmed sufficiently to allow summer ice loss to exceed winter accumulations. That glacial "tipping point" occurred around 1800, with full-on retreat by 1820. Thus began two centuries of worldwide glacial retreat that continues today. Notwithstanding man's influence on climate in recent decades, there has been *no acceleration* in the rate of retreat.

The glaciers began to recede at least a century before appreciable quantities of man-made CO_2 began to accumulate in the atmosphere and nearly a century before the Mann-made Hockey Stick showed warming had started.

One more nail in the climate alarmists' coffin.

Sea level and glaciation go hand in hand. When water is locked up in the ice of glacial advances, sea level drops. Conversely, warming and the glacial retreat that comes with it return water chiefly to the oceans, raising sea level. Again, we see that the rising sea level began a century before the IPCC and Michael Mann tell us it should have occurred (Figure. I-26).

Conclusive evidence from multiple lines of reasoning shows that, contrary to Michael Mann's hockey-stick graph, warming began 300 years ago and marked the beginning of the end of the Little Ice Age.

Was this warming unusual or unprecedented? Figure I-27 is a compilation of reconstructed temperature histories using a variety of proxy sources including ice cores and lake sediments. Loehle (2008) compiled 18 peer-reviewed studies of 2,000-year-long data series using sources other than tree-rings. (The author believed that

Figure I-25: 200 years of glacial retreat

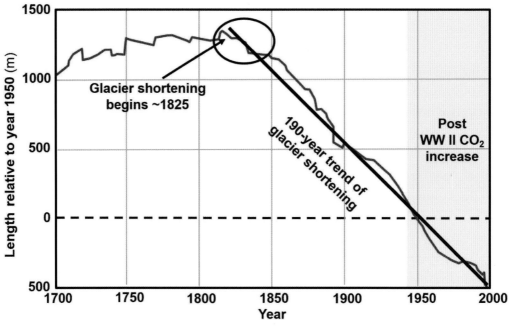

(Source data: Oerlemans 2005)

Figure I-26: Greater than 200 years of sea-level rise

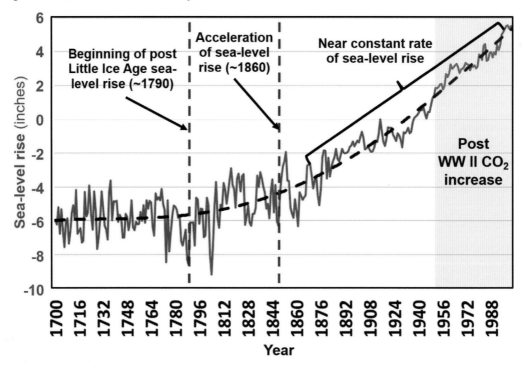

(Source data: Jevrejeva 2008, PSMSL 2008)

the tree-ring data such as those used by Dr. Mann for his hockey stick could not accurately capture long-term climate changes, and so excluded tree-ring data from his summary.)

In direct contradiction of Mann's hockey stick, Dr. Loehle's data confirmed not only that the Medieval Warm Period and the Little Ice Age existed but also that the current warming trend began more than 300 years ago, just as the Central England data in Figure I-24 show.

He concluded that his compilation of proxies:

> *...shows the Medieval Warm Period (MWP) and Little Ice Age (LIA) quite clearly, with the MWP being approximately 0.3°C warmer than 20th-century values at these 18 sites.*

Figure I-27: 2,000 years of temperature data

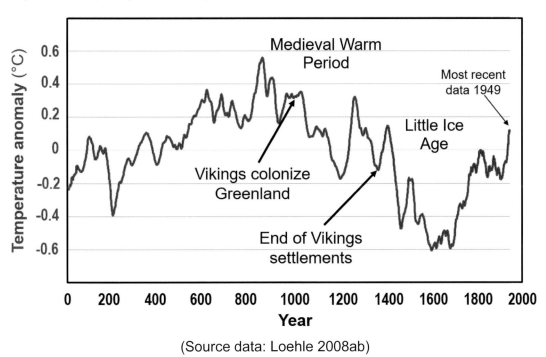

(Source data: Loehle 2008ab)

Placing recent warming into the framework of longer datasets is a key to understanding whether our modern temperatures are similar to past climate events, rather than being an unusual occurrence. Fortunately, we have quite detailed and accurate temperature data from the Antarctica and Greenland ice cores. In Antarctica, the data reach back 810,000 years, while in Greenland several ice cores provide valuable data for more than 150,000 years.

Since this book is for non-scientists, we shall not go into the details of how temperatures are calculated using ice data. Briefly, the ratio of two isotopes of oxygen is used as a guide to the temperature of the air at the time when it was trapped by the weight of snow above it. The scientific basis for temperature predictions using this method is solid and has been verified with comparisons to known recent temperatures.

Let us first look at the most extensive ice-core history available. It was retrieved from ice core drilling in Antarctica. Figure I-28 represents 800,000 years of temperature data. The 100,000-year cycles of ice ages and interglacial warm periods show up clearly.

Figure I-28: The ups and downs of temperature over the past 800,000 years

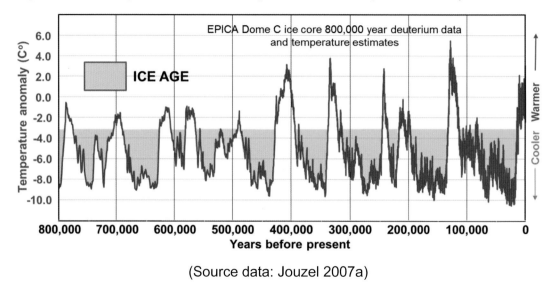

(Source data: Jouzel 2007a)

Inconvenient Fact 14

Temperatures have changed for 800,000 years. It wasn't us.
(This Inconvenient Fact deserves to be repeated often.)

The periods of glaciation last for 70,000 – 125,000 years, while the warmer interglacials last 10,000 to 15,000 years. Importantly, we are now about 11,000 years into our current interglacial period, which may end within the next century or last another several thousand years. In any case, the beneficial interglacial warmth that we are enjoying now will end at some point in the not too distant future (in a geologic sense). When that next ice age descends upon us, it will be a true climate apocalypse accompanied by crop failures, famine, mass emigration from colder to warmer regions and unprecedented population loss.

The next ice age could arrive at any time… Don't sell your parka.

Inconvenient Fact 15

Interglacials usually last 10,000 – 15,000 years. Ours is 11,000 years old.

A closer look at the last four glacial cycles dating back 400,000 years is still more revealing (Figure I-29). Now the inconvenient facts start to pile up.

Figure I-29: The ups and downs of temperature over the past 400,000 years

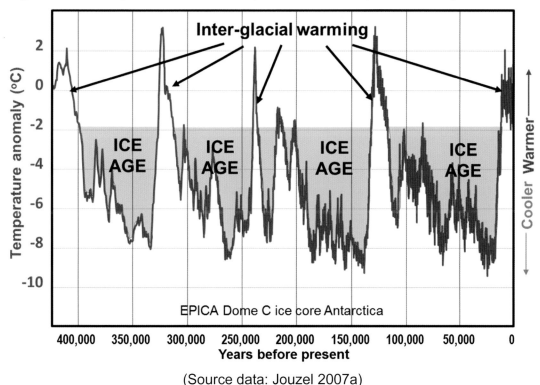

(Source data: Jouzel 2007a)

Inconvenient Fact 16

Each of the four previous inter-glacial warming periods was significantly warmer than our current temperature.

Inconvenient Fact 17

The last interglacial, ~120,000 years ago, was 8°C (14°F) warmer than today. The polar bears survived. Greenland didn't melt.

Recent research by the Niels Bohr Institute (Dahl-Jensen 2013) was the first to target ice accumulated in Greenland during the previous interglacial period, known as the Eemian. The results are very inconvenient for those promoting climate doom. The results revealed that the Eemian interglacial warm period, between 130,000 and 115,000 years ago, was much warmer than previously thought. In fact, it was, 8°C (14.4°F) warmer than today. The implications are enormous.

Even though the temperatures during the Eemian were 2.5°C (4.5°F) higher than even the most aggressive IPCC predictions, the Greenland ice sheet lost only a quarter of its mass. While 25% is significant, it is far less than the alarmist predictions of total ice elimination in response to far less warming. Also, polar bears evolved about 150,000 years ago and survived the Eemian warm period even though there was seldom any polar ice. That fact alone discredits theories of a pending polar-bear extinction caused by moderate man-made warming.

The most recent IPCC Summary Report predicted complete destruction of the Greenland ice sheet in response to much less warming than during the Eemian:

> *Models project that a local annual-average warming of larger than 3°C sustained for millennia would lead to virtually a complete melting of the Greenland ice sheet.*

Or not.

Figure I-30 is a closer look at the last 10,000 years of data from the Greenland Ice Sheet Project (GISP2) reaching back to the beginning of our current interglacial period. This chart should finally convince you that the global warming scare is just that, a fanciful hobgoblin profitable to its inventors and cripplingly expensive to the rest of us.

If Michael Mann, Al Gore and other promoters of climate catastrophe cannot show that the current warming trend is "unusual and unprecedented", they have no cause for the alarm they are sowing. Figure I-30 may be the most substantial piece of evidence that the modern warming is neither unusual nor unprecedented. Rather, it is very similar to nine other warming trends of the last 10,000 years. This chart, in which the present temperature for a coring site known as GISP2 is estimated from the work of researchers at Ohio State University (Box 2009), should be first on your list of "why global-warming alarmists are wrong."

Figure I-30: 10,000 years of blessed warmth

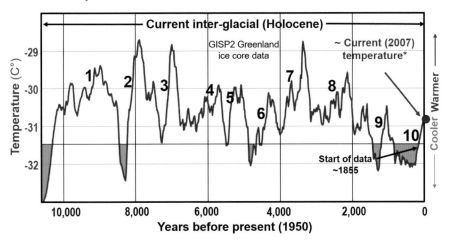

(Source data: temperature: Alley 2004; current temperature: Box 2009)

The damning data show that, for more than 6,100 years (or 60%) of the current interglacial warm period, the temperature was warmer than it is today. Of the nine earlier significant periods of warming since the end of the last ice age, five had *higher rates* of temperature increase (Figure I-31) and seven had *larger total increases* in temperature. Moreover, each of the previous warming cycles experienced significantly higher temperatures than today. It should be clear, based on this chart, that our current warming trend is a natural and predictable result of our fortunate exit out of the Little Ice Age.

Unusual? Unprecedented? No and no.

From these 10,000 years of data, the inconvenient facts now come fast and furious:

Inconvenient Fact 18

Temperatures changed during the past 10,000 years. It wasn't us.

Inconvenient Fact 19

Today's total warming and warming rate are similar to earlier periods.

Inconvenient Fact 20

It was warmer than today for 6,100 of the last 10,000 years.

Inconvenient Fact 21

The current warming trend is neither unusual nor unprecedented.

Figure I-31: Five earlier warming periods had higher rates of warming than today.

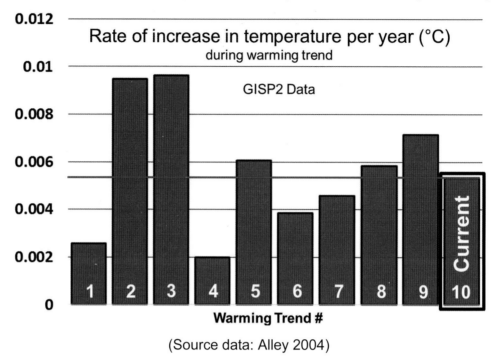

(Source data: Alley 2004)

Temperature is rarely constant. It is either rising or falling, and quite substantially at that. There have been nine significant previous warming trends over the last 10,000 years. These warming trends are similar to today's, but each ended with much higher temperatures than today's. Even if you slept through your history classes, you might recall that there were no SUVs or coal-fired power plants operating in China during these previous warming periods, yet temperatures rose and fell anyway. The warming and cooling of the Earth have natural causes, and those natural causes did not suddenly halt at the start of the Industrial Revolution.

If the past is the signpost to the future, we will see some more naturally driven warming before we go back into the next cooling cycle. For the sake of mankind, let us hope that the next cooling trend will not happen too soon, and will not take us into the next ice age.

Stepping Millions of Years Back in Time

The ice-core data revealed much about how our current temperature trend compares with others since the present era of 100,000-year glaciation cycles began. Five million years of data (Lisiecki 2005) show that, overall, our planet has experienced a long decline in temperatures. Beginning 3.5 million years ago, a series of 45 ice ages began.

This long period of increasing cold began with ice ages on a 41,000-year cycle and included 33 separate glacial events. For the last 1.25 million years we have been in a more severe 100,000 year-cycle in which, during 13 ice ages, there were glaciations lasting typically 90,000 years and interglacial warm periods lasting about 10,000 years (Carter 2011).

Inconvenient Fact 22

Earth's orbit and tilt drive glacial-interglacial changes.

The glacial-interglacial cycles are controlled by changes in the Earth's tilt and the shape of its orbit that occur in predictable cycles. The eccentricity of the Earth's elliptical orbit (i.e., how far the shape of the orbit differs from a perfect circle) varies in 100,000-year cycles. The tilt or obliquity of the Earth's axis varies in 41,000-year cycles. The Earth also wobbles on a 26,000-year cycle that causes a phenomenon known as the "precession of the equinoxes". Collectively, these three cycles, which were originally discovered by a self-taught university janitor named James Croll, are now known as the Milankovich cycles.

These long-term astronomical changes indicate that changes in CO_2 concentration cannot have been the chief reason for warming and cooling in geological time.

Figure I-32 provides additional confirmation that we should be more concerned about a continuation of the multi-million-year downward trend in temperature, rather than fretting over the welcome warmth over the last 150 years.

Figure I-32: 3.5 million years of declining temperature

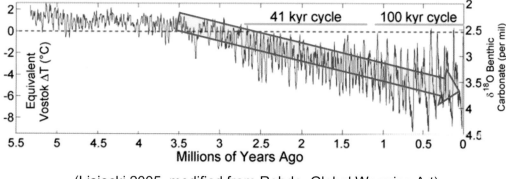

(Lisiecki 2005, modified from Rohde, Global Warming Art)

Figure I-33 shows 65 million years of temperature data from oxygen isotope records of deep ocean sediment cores. For the bulk of this time, Earth was so warm that there was no ice at either pole. Only in the relatively recent past has there been any ice at the northern pole. Based on this data, we are living within the coldest period in the last 65 million years (Robinson 2012).

You will hear from the proponents of catastrophic warming that our temperatures are unusual and unprecedented. They are absolutely right: *we are living in times that are unusually cold!*

Figure I-33: For 65 million years, the weather was warmer than today.

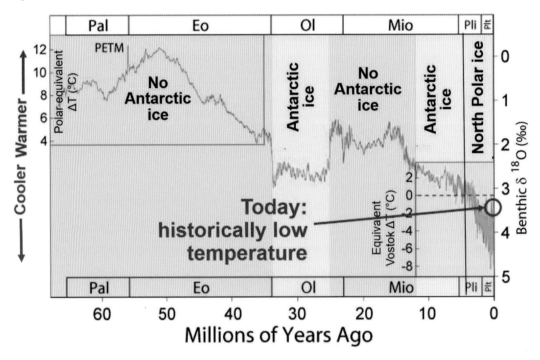

(Zachos 2001, modified from Rohde, Global Warming Art)

Figure I-34, showing more than 4 billion years' temperature data as adapted from Scotese (2002), reveals that the Earth is now in one of the coldest periods in its history. No geological period has been as cold as our current geologic period, the Quaternary, for at least 250 million years.

Temperature variations of more than 10°C (18°F) in either direction have been common. Viewed in the context of millions of years of Earth history, our recent increase of 0.8°C (1.4°F) appears minuscule. It barely registers as a blip on the chart.

Figure I-34: Four billion years of temperature data

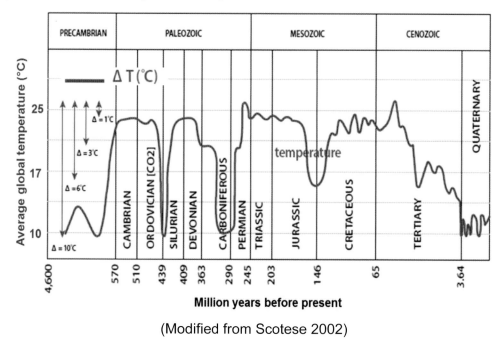

(Modified from Scotese 2002)

The inconvenient facts continue to come at a rapid pace based on this long-term data:

Inconvenient Fact 23

We are living in one of the coldest periods in all of Earth's history.

Inconvenient Fact 24

Earth has not had a geologic period this cold in 250 million years.

Inconvenient Fact 25

The only thing constant about temperatures over 600 million years is that they have been constantly changing.
(This is a recurring Inconvenient Fact.)

Inconvenient Fact 26

For most of Earth's history, it was about 10°C (18°F) warmer than today.

Our review of these four billion years of data shows that the Earth usually has been either very warm or very cold, oscillating between very warm "hothouse" conditions and much colder "icehouse" or "snowball Earth" conditions. During hothouse periods, high temperatures prevail and ice is rare. During icehouse periods such as the present, the Earth cycles between long periods of glaciation and shorter interglacial periods of somewhat warmer temperatures, but with extensive ice at both poles. The current "icehouse" phase has lasted 3.5 million years. Fortunately for mankind, we are currently in a blessedly warm interglacial period. For that, we should be thankful.

Figure I-35: Icehouse to hothouse fluctuations

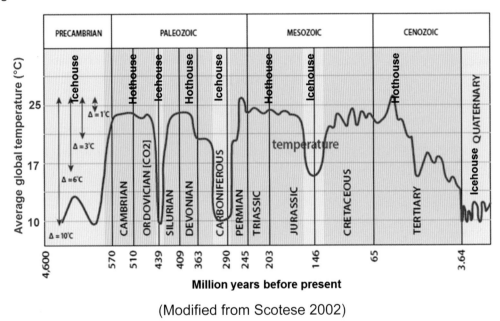

(Modified from Scotese 2002)

Climate Models: Accurate, Inaccurate or Useless?

The data don't matter. We're not basing our recommendations [for reductions in carbon dioxide emissions] upon the data. We're basing them upon the climate models.

— Chris Folland, U.K. Meteorological Office

Rather than seeing models as describing literal truth, we ought to see them as convenient fictions which try to provide something useful.

— David Frame, climate modeler, Oxford University

A recent paper by Bjorn Lomborg, an economist, estimated that the cost of measures to forestall global warming would be $1.5 trillion per year. What are the expected results from this expenditure?

According to Lomborg's calculations using the MAGICC simulator, by 2100 (on the optimistic assumption that every nation on Earth adhered to its climate commitments) temperatures will have been reduced in his best case by 0.17°C (0.31°F). That is less than half of a degree Fahrenheit, or $42 trillion for each reduction of one-tenth of a degree Fahrenheit in global temperature. Methinks that might not be a very good investment.

Why are we planning to spend this outrageous amount of money that might be used instead to help lift people out of generational poverty? It is based on mathematically complicated climate models that predict a significant rise in future temperatures, accompanied with an imagined host of climate hobgoblins. As we shall see in the chapters on the many myths of climate apocalypse, none of these predicted doomsday events are evident today. If we are to base our policy decisions on predictive models, we should find out if the models are actually able to accurately forecast future temperatures.

A detailed examination by John Christy, a distinguished climatologist at the University of Alabama at Huntsville and Alabama State Climatologist, provides a stark assessment of the validity (or non-validity) of the models that are used in support of imagined apocalypse. His testimony in February 2016 to the U.S. House Committee on Science, Space & Technology included remarkable charts that document just how much the models overestimate temperatures.

The red line in Fig. I-36 shows the average of 102 climate model runs completed by Christy and his team at the University of Alabama in Huntsville using the models on which IPCC itself relies. Also shown on the chart are the actual, observed temperatures. *The models exaggerate warming, on average, two and a half times the actual temperature* (or three times over in the climate-crucial tropics).

Inconvenient Fact 27

IPCC models have overstated warming up to three times too much.

Supporting Christy's findings, Patrick Michaels, Director for the Study of Science at the Cato Institute, studied a suite of 108 climate model runs dating back to 1984 and used in the 2013 IPCC compendium. He found that the models predicted a warming rate of 2.6°C (4.7°F) per century versus 1.7°C (3.1°F) in the real world. That is a big difference.

Figure I-36: Global warming predicted by models compared with real-world warming

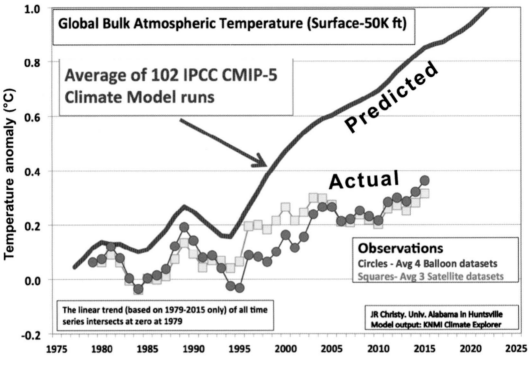

(Modified from Christy 2016)

We are relying on complex computer programs, using an array of complicated equations "tweaked" by the scientists who built them to arrive at a forecast temperature some 100 years into the future. We cannot confidently forecast temperature merely 10 days in the future from now, but are asked to base climate policies and risk trillions of dollars on models that have failed and failed again the test of prediction versus observation.

> *Applied to the climate, a very slight error in the boundary conditions*
> *(for example, the movement of a butterfly's wing) would be escalated by*
> *the equations, making a long term forecast impossible.*
> > — Dr. Edward Lorenz: father of chaos theory
> > on the use of current climate models

> *In climate research and modelling, we should recognize that we are*
> *dealing with a coupled non-linear chaotic system, and therefore that*
> *the long-term prediction of future climate states is not possible.*
> > — IPCC (2001, §14.2.2.2)

Winter's Coming — Is Another Ice Age on its Way?

We are now more than 10,000 years into our current interglacial warm period, and these warm periods typically last 10,000 – 15,000 years. We see from Figure I-37 that temperatures have been in a more than 3,500-year decline, and that the peak temperature of each of the last three warm periods was less than that of the period that preceded it. Might this data be telling us to get ready for the onset of true glaciation? The author of reconstructed histories of temperature from an Antarctic core concluded: "The Holocene [our present inter-glacial period], which has already lasted 11,000 years, is, by far, the longest stable warm period recorded in Antarctica during the past 420,000 years" (Petit 1999). You may want to consider buying an extra set of mittens or, better yet, some property in Costa Rica.

An arrival of the next ice age would be a horrific catastrophe for human civilization. If the most recent glacial advances are an indicator of what we may see in the future (Figure I-38), prospects for humanity in much of the northern hemisphere are bleak. Large portions of North America and Europe will be covered in many hundreds or thousands of feet of ice. Colder temperatures will cause massive crop failures and famine, and mass migration from cold to warm would be inevitable.

Figure I-37: 3,500 years of falling temperature

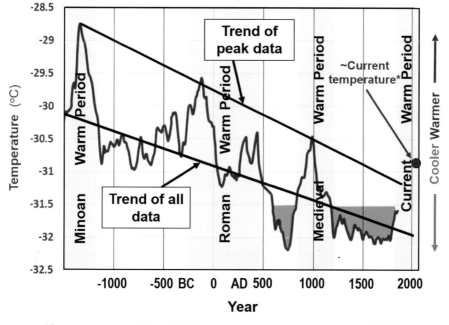

(Source data: Alley 2004: present temperature Box 2009)

Figure I-38: Icy problems ahead for more than 120 million in North America alone

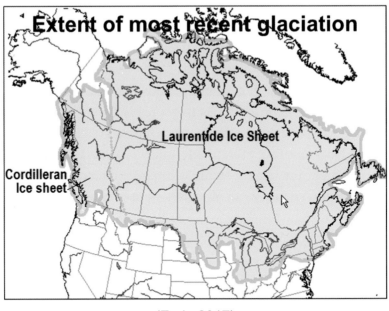

(Earle 2017)

It would take only a few years of global crop failure from cold weather to cause tens of millions of deaths worldwide. In North America alone, ice would eventually cover areas that are now home to 85 million people in the United States and another 35 million in Canada. Nearly all of Canada and most of the Scandinavian countries might eventually need to be abandoned to the ice.

Would it not be ironic if we spent trillions of dollars on CO_2 mitigation only to realize in the not too distant future that we should have been doing the opposite?

As we shall see in the next section, history tells us that each warming period over the last several thousand years ended very badly with the subsequent cooling, usually with widespread loss of life and a decline in the human condition.

It is somewhat ironic that our contribution of greenhouse gases to the
atmosphere may actually be helping to delay the next ice age from starting!
                                            — United States Geological Survey (USGS)

Climate and Culture: Very Good and Very Bad

Human advancement, from the cave-dwelling mammoth hunter during the last ice age to the modern millennial using a smart-phone app while riding in a self-driving Audi, happens in fits and starts. Nearly all great advances occurred during warm periods. Conversely, during cold periods, the human condition declined.

Before climate science became politicized, warm periods were referred to by scientists as "climate optima" because, for almost all species on Earth, warmer is better than colder.

During the 100,000 years of the most recent Ice Age, human civilization barely advanced. Our ancestors relied on a subsistence culture of hunting and gathering, using what was available in their immediate area. Limited advances were made in flint-knapping or cave-painting, but civilization barely advanced. A little over 10,000 years ago, all that changed. The growing warmth at the end of the ice age enabled humanity to prosper and advance. Domestication of animals and the birth of agriculture led to an explosion of population and the creation of the first communities.

The most dramatic advances in civilization took place during the last four warm periods—including our own (Figure I-39). The advancement of science, technology and the arts have been directly linked to warmer weather. The warming, which made possible an abundance of food, freed the population from its preoccupation with daily survival to do other things. It led to cultural development, something impossible during the cold periods.

The recurring theme of civilization's relationship with climate provides the context for our next Inconvenient Fact:

Inconvenient Fact 28

For human advancement, warmer is better than colder.

The Minoan Warm Period (1,500 – 1,200 BC) coincided with what is known as the Bronze Age. In this period, humanity saw great early advancements such as the invention of the wheel, writing, bronze-smelting, and wine-making. Mountain passes became accessible and storms abated, allowing trade throughout Europe and the Mediterranean. Great cities arose. The first great European and Egyptian civilizations arose early in this period, including the Mycenaean culture in Greece, and the first great Egyptian dynasties, among those, the reign of the Pharaoh Akhenaten.

Figure I-39: 4,000 years of temperature-driven cultural advances and retreats

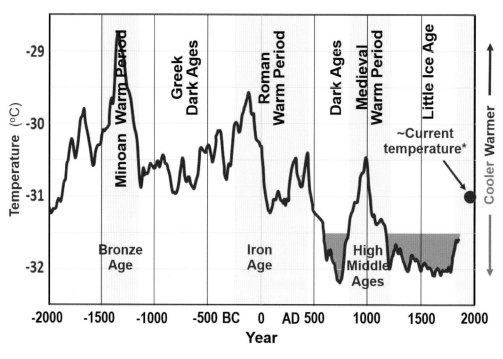

(Source data: Alley 2004; *current temperature Box 2009)

As we saw earlier, scientific measurements from ice and sediment cores indicate that the Minoan Warm Period was much hotter than today. This Inconvenient Fact is supported by historical documentation such the growing of millet as far north as Scandinavia—an activity that occurs today only in tropical or subtropical regions.

Minoan prosperity was followed by the significantly lower temperatures and the consequent decline in the human condition known to climatologists as the "Vandal Minimum" and in Greek history as the "Greek Dark Ages." During the Vandal Minimum, mere survival was the prevailing endeavor. Crop failures led to undernourishment and population loss. The cold period persisted from 1,200 – 250 BC, but things went from bad to worse around 800 BC when temperatures plunged even lower and a new round of depopulation occurred across Europe. This time is known as the "Hallstatt Disaster" (Behringer 2007).

The Roman Warm Period, also known as the "Roman Optimum," (~250 BC to 450 AD) witnessed a beneficial rise in temperature and ushered in the explosion of civilization known as the Iron Age. This period saw tremendous growth in mathematics, philosophy, the arts and agriculture. Expansion of societies across Europe and Asia occurred, including the apex of the Roman Empire and the first of the great Chinese empires (Han Dynasty).

Multiple lines of scientific study drawing evidence from sources such as sediments, ice cores and pollen from around the world have documented that the Roman Warm Period was not only hotter than today, but significantly so. Voluminous historical records confirm the warmth as well, as does the presence of olive trees and vineyards much farther to the north than can presently be grown. Olives grew as far north as the Rhine Valley of Germany, and citrus trees in the north of England near Hadrian's Wall.

The rise in civilization during the Roman Warm Period was followed by a devastating cold era (~450 to 950 AD), which ushered in one of the bleakest times in modern history: the Dark Ages. This era was characterized by famine, the Black Plague and a great decline in the population of Europe. The cold and its associated maladies devastated the cities, reducing much of Europe to a largely rural-agricultural existence. Survival again took precedence over the advancement of civilization.

This time of cold coincided with the decline and fall of the two major empires of the preceding warm period—the Roman and Han Empires. While it may not be entirely accurate to blame climate for the decline of both of these and other lesser civilizations, the inability of rulers to feed their subjects led to tremendous internal strife, including uprisings and political turmoil.

The Medieval Warm Period (950 to 1250 AD) ushered in the great awakening of the "High Middle Ages." The associated positive environmental conditions are often

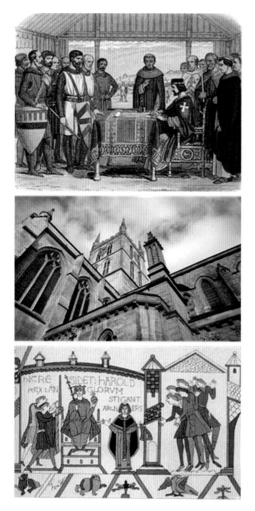

called the "Little Climatic Optimum." This period of warmth saw an intellectual renaissance, the establishment of universities, the building of great castles and cathedrals, settlements on Iceland and Greenland and the signing of the Magna Carta. Charles Doren, the historian, called it "...one of the most optimistic, prosperous and progressive periods in European history" (Moore 1996).

Recall that Dr. Mann and the IPCC dispute even the existence of the Medieval Warm Period (MWP). To admit its existence would be to cast doubt on their contention that we are living in an unusually warm time. Prior to the Mann hockey stick, the warmth of the MWP was undisputed, backed up by extensive historical documentation of tree lines, agriculture, insects, glaciers and pollen, all supporting the thesis of the MWP being warmer than today.

Documentation of the Medieval Warm Period is voluminous and includes evidence of citrus fruits and vineyards located much farther north than at present and burial sites of Vikings still lying in permafrost in Greenland. A superb collection of historical and scientific studies that bolster the notion of a much warmer MWP can be found at the website CO2Science.org run by the Center for the Study of Carbon Dioxide and Global Change.

Near the end of the MWP, those enjoying the benefits of the warmth little realized that there would soon be more than half a millennium of cold, misery, and death.

Bad things happen during cold periods. No period in history demonstrates this fact more than the period that followed the Medieval Warm Period—the Little Ice Age. From about 1250 – 1850, the cold brought severe hardship primarily in northern latitudes. The combination of bitterly cold winters and cool, wet summers led to crop failure, famine and severe population decline. The worst of the cold occurred during the deep freeze from 1670 – 1715, a period of extreme cold known as the Maunder Minimum.

During the Little Ice Age, the Baltic Sea froze over and shipping to Iceland and Greenland became impossible for long periods. The Vikings abandoned Greenland in about 1350, and the population of Iceland was halved. The Black Death (1348) and the Great Famine (1315 – 1321) occurred early in this period.

> *And what a wonder! Some knights who were sitting on a magnificently outfitted horse gave the horse and their weapons away for cheap wine; and they did so because they were so terribly hungry.*
> — A German chronicler of 1315 (Jordan 1996)

In Norse mythology there is reference to a *Fimbulwinter*—a three-year winter with no intervening summer. This is thought to reference extreme cold periods that occurred early in the Little Ice. Age. Temperatures in England were so low that the Thames River often froze solid. The last time the Thames froze was in 1814. The North Atlantic fishing industry was devastated by the demise of the cod population. Recall also the cold suffered by General Washington's troops during the winter at Valley Forge.

The beginning of the end of the Little Ice Age occurred with a rapid warming from 1695 – 1735 in Central England at a rate equivalent to >4 degrees Celsius per century. That warming, which occurred naturally and which we cannot have caused, continues to this day, though at a gentler pace. No 40-year period since then has seen so great a rate of warming. Most researchers determine the end of the Little Ice Age to be around 1850, but, as we have seen, it could just as easily be assigned a date 100 years or more earlier, long before any human CO_2 could have been an influence.

Civilization at the end of the Little Ice Age had progressed little since the time of the High Middle Ages. It was mostly agricultural. The horse was the primary means of transport. Communication was by word of mouth or by letter.

Yet, in less than 150 years we have progressed to a level of advancement that could not have been imagined only 50 years ago, all during rising temperatures and increasing carbon dioxide levels. Author W. Cleon Skousen called this rapid advancement the "5,000 Year Leap," where 5,000 years of advances in communication, transportation, energy, and exploration, and a doubling of the average length of human life, were condensed into less than 200 years. A myriad of factors were responsible, but it is certainly not clear that they would have occurred had we still been mired in the frigid temperatures of the Little Ice Age.

We should be thankful that we are the beneficiaries of the warmer weather. It allows us to tinker, to invent, and to dream, without the daily worries of finding our next meal.

There is, perhaps, a 97% consensus among historians that, contrary to what Dr. Michael Mann and the IPCC contend, the Little Ice Age actually occurred and that the Roman, Medieval and Minoan Warming Periods were warmer than today. Hundreds of scientific papers and thousands of historic accounts confirm this Inconvenient Fact.

Perhaps it is time that Dr. Mann and his fellow climate travelers were labeled "history deniers."

Summary

Contrary to what the promoters of climate doom would have us believe, extensive historic and scientific studies document that the temperature increase over the last one hundred or so years is neither unusual nor unprecedented. We have also seen that, rather than a pending climate apocalypse, the modern warming should be viewed as a welcome respite from the troubles and cold of the previous centuries and one that is remarkably similar to many previous such trends in our current interglacial period.

One of the primary complaints of those agitating for a reduction in CO_2 emissions is that the weather has become warmer since the Industrial Revolution. Although it goes unstated, climate alarmists apparently believe that the ideal temperature for today would be that of the time before the beginning of the Industrial Revolution. That would put us squarely in the middle of the temperatures of the Little Ice Age. History does not support any such belief.

Cold, death and pestilence is what history tells us accompanies lower temperatures. Is that what the scientists, politicians and environmental alarmists agitating for less CO_2 want? Do they really want to return to the temperatures of the Little Ice Age, the Dark Ages or the Greek Dark Ages? We have seen how poorly our civilization fared during those cold periods. A return to lower temperatures likely would result in a decimation of the human population. But then, isn't that what many of the climate zealots really want?

The extinction of the human species may not only be inevitable but a good thing.
— Christopher Manes, a writer for Earth First! Journal

Inconvenient Fact 29

A return to the temperature at the beginning of the Industrial Revolution would lead to famine and death.

II. Apocalypse? No! — Climate Apocalypse Myths

Weather Gone Wild

Rains that are almost biblical, heat waves that don't end, tornadoes that strike in savage swarms—there's been a change in the weather lately. What's going on?

— National Geographic 2011

My, oh, my, the sky is falling. I must run and tell the lion about it.

— Chicken Little

In the early days of the climate alarmist campaign, the focus was nearly entirely on effects directly related to a warming climate: heat waves, droughts, rising sea-levels and the like. In the mid-2000s, with the realization that "global warming" had mysteriously stopped or at least paused, a new group of climate hobgoblins was conjured up under the term *climate change*. Now anything at all unusual or harmful could be demonized and linked to our sins of emission. And demonize them they have.

A whole host of climate myths have been advanced to further the notion that humankind is not only changing the climate, but that those changes are devastating the planet and dragging down the human condition with it. Supposed climate calamities linked to man's actions run the gamut, from forest fires to the spread of poison ivy. The linkage has one goal: to instill fear so that we will welcome the imposition of radical, costly regulations on our lives.

It certainly seems like extreme events are more frequent. With assistance from a 24-hour news cycle, Twitter, Google updates and cell phone alerts, we are barraged with weather events that formerly merited coverage only in local news outlets. Now a tornado that touches down in Valdosta, Georgia, may be publicized worldwide instead of only in the Daily Times.

One can hardly blame the media for coverage, as most of these events make for fantastic live shots of forests in flame and homes ablaze. Mild weather just does not make for good television.

Even many of those reading this book who are skeptical of a human link to a warming planet believe that climate catastrophes are increasing in number and intensity. And why would they not? It is regularly reported as a fact that "extreme" weather is more prevalent, along with wide-eyed predictions of even more such ruinous events, owing to a warming world.

The following chapters provide information on many of the primary climate myths, most of which you will find completely at odds with portrayals in the media, and possibly with your own understanding. We will look first at the most pervasive myth, that of a scientific consensus on climate change. We then "dive deep" into the myths of a climate apocalypse.

You will find that, rather than living in a world careening toward planetary doom because of our excesses, just the opposite is the case. Humanity and the Earth are prospering wildly, not *in spite* of rising temperatures and increasing carbon dioxide, but *because* of them.

The Earth is becoming greener and experiencing fewer extreme weather events. Lengthening growing seasons, more moisture in the soil, and CO_2 fertilization are increasing crop yields. With these increases, we are feeding our growing populations.

Enjoy the inconvenient truth and sleep well: the world as we know it is not ending because of your actions.

Apocalypse? No!

"97% Consensus" — What Consensus?

We have heard that 97% of scientists agree on human-driven climate change. You may also have heard that those who don't buy into the climate-apocalypse mantra are Luddite science-deniers. So count me in as a Luddite, but a whole lot more than 3% of scientists are skeptical of the party line on climate. A whole lot more.

In most conversations that I have with people who learn that I am a scientist working on climate change, the first question that comes up is, "So you believe in climate change, then?" My answer? "Yes, of course I do: it has been happening for hundreds of millions of years." As you know by now, the question is not, "Is climate change happening?" The real question is, "Is climate change now driven primarily by human actions?"

There are some scientific truths that are quantifiable and easily proven, and with which, I am confident, at least 97% of scientists agree. Here are two:

> Carbon dioxide concentration has been increasing in recent years.
> Temperatures, as measured by thermometers and satellites, have been generally increasing over the last 150 years.

What is impossible to quantify is the actual percentage of warming that is attributable to increased anthropogenic (human-caused) CO_2. There is no scientific evidence or method that can determine how much of the warming we've had since 1900 was directly caused by us.

We know that temperature has varied greatly over the millennia. We also know that for virtually all of that time, global warming and cooling were driven entirely by natural forces, which did not cease to operate at the beginning of the Industrial Revolution.

The claim that most modern warming is attributable to human activities is scientifically insupportable. The truth is that we do not know. We need to be able to separate what we *do* know from that which is only conjecture.

What is the basis for the "97% consensus" notion? Is it true?

Hint: You can't spell consensus without "con."

If, indeed, 97% of all scientists truly believed that human activities were causing the moderate warming that we have seen in the last 150 years, it would be reasonable for one to consider this when determining what to believe. One would be wrong, however.

Science, unlike religion, is not a belief system. Scientists, just like anyone else, will say that they believe things (whether they believe them or not) for social convenience, political expediency or financial profit. For this and other good reasons, science is not founded upon the beliefs of scientists. It is a disciplined method of inquiry, by which the scientist applies pre-existing theory to observation and measurement, so as to develop or to reject a theory, so that he can unravel as clearly and as certainly as possible the distinction between what the Greek philosopher Anaximander called "that which is and that which is not."

Abu Ali ibn al-Haytham, the natural philosopher of 11th-century Iraq who founded the scientific method in the East, once wrote:

> *The seeker after truth [his beautiful description of the scientist] does not place his faith in any mere consensus, however venerable or widespread. Instead, he subjects what he has learned of it to inquiry, inspection and investigation. The road to the truth is long and hard, but that is the road we must follow.*

The long and hard road to scientific truth cannot be followed by the trivial expedient of a mere head-count among those who make their livings from government funding. Therefore, the mere fact that climate activists find themselves so often appealing to an imagined and (as we shall see) imaginary "consensus" is a red flag. They are far less sure of the supposed scientific truths to which they cling than they would like us to believe. "Consensus," here, is a crutch for lame science.

What, then, is the origin of the "97% consensus" notion? Is it backed up with research and data?

The earliest attempt to document a "consensus" on climate change was a 2004 paper cited by Al Gore in his allegedly non-fiction book, *An Inconvenient Truth.* (Gore attended natural science class at Harvard, but got a D grade for it.) The author of the cited paper, Naomi Oreskes, asserted that 75% of nearly 1,000 papers she had reviewed on the question of climate change agreed with the "consensus" proposition favored by the IPCC: "Most of the observed warming over the last 50 years is likely to have been due to the increase in greenhouse gas concentrations." None, she maintained, dissented from this line of reasoning.

The Oreskes paper came to the attention of Klaus-Martin Schulte, an eminent London surgeon, who had become concerned with the adverse health effects of his patients from their belief in apocalyptic global warming.

Professor Schulte decided to update Oreskes' work. However, he found that only 45% of several hundred papers endorsed the "consensus" position. He concluded: "There appears to be little basis in the peer-reviewed scientific literature for the degree of alarm on the issue of climate change which is being expressed in the media and by politicians, now carried over into the medical world and experienced by patients."

The primary paper that is often trotted out in support of the notion of "97% consensus" was written by John Cook and his merry band of climate extremists. Published in 2013, it is the most widely referenced work on the subject of climate consensus and has been downloaded more than 600,000 times.

Cook runs a climate website that is a smorgasbord of alarmist rhetoric, specializing in attacks—often personal and spiteful in tone—on all who have proven effective in leading others to stray from the dogma of impending climate doom.

The project was self-described as "a 'citizen science' project by volunteers contributing to the website." The team consisted of 12 climate activists who did not leave their climate prejudices at home. These volunteers, many of whom had no training in the sciences, said they had "reviewed" abstracts from 11,944 peer-reviewed papers related to climate change or global warming, published over the 21 years 1991 – 2011, to assess the extent to which they supported the "consensus view" on climate change. As Cook's paper said,

We analysed a large sample of the scientific literature on global CC [climate change], published over a 21-year period, in order to determine the level of scientific consensus that human activity is very likely causing most of the current GW (anthropogenic global warming, or AGW). ...

The paper concluded,

Among abstracts that expressed a position on AGW [anthropogenic global warming], 97.1% endorsed the scientific consensus. ... Among papers expressing a position on AGW, an overwhelming percentage (97.2% based on self-ratings, 97.1% based on abstract ratings) endorses the scientific consensus on AGW.

The paper asserted—falsely, as it turned out—that 97% of the papers the reviewers examined had explicitly endorsed the opinion that humans are causing the majority of the warming of the last 150 years.

When one looks at the data, one finds that 7,930 of the papers took no position at all on the subject and were arbitrarily excluded from the count on this ground. If we simply add back all of the papers reviewed, the 97% claimed by Cook and his co-authors falls to 32.6%.

A closer look at the paper reveals that the so-called "97%" included three categories of endorsement of human-caused climate change (Table II-1). Only the first category amounted to an explicit statement that humans are the primary cause of recent warming. The second and third categories would include most skeptics of catastrophic anthropogenic warming, including me, who accept that increasing CO_2 is probably causing some, probably small, amount of warming; an amount that is likely rendered insignificant by natural causes of warmer weather.

Table II-1: Expanding the 'consensus' broadly

Level of Endorsement	Description
(1) Explicit endorsement with quantification	Explicitly states that humans are the primary cause of recent global warming
(2) Explicit endorsement without quantification	Explicitly states that humans are causing global warming or refers to anthropogenic global warming/climate change as a known fact
(3) Implicit endorsement	Implies humans are causing global warming; e.g. research assumes greenhouse gas emissions cause warming without explicitly stating humans are the cause

Cook (2013)

Michael Bastasch wrote in 2017 that lumping skeptics with true climate change devotees was "like claiming there's a consensus on legalized abortion by lumping pro-abortion activists in with those who oppose all abortion except in cases of incest and rape. That 'consensus' would be a meaningless talking point."

Agnotology is defined as "the study of how ignorance arises via circulation of misinformation calculated to mislead." This is how David Legates and his co-authors (2015) describe the Cook paper and similar attempts falsely to promote the notion of broad scientific consensus surrounding the subject of a looming, man-made, climate apocalypse.

They reviewed the actual papers used by Cook and found that *only 0.3% of the 11,944 abstracts and 1.6% of the smaller sample that excluded those papers expressing no opinion endorsed man-made global warming as they defined it.* Remarkably, they found that Cook and his assistants had themselves marked only 64 papers—or 0.5% of the 11,944 they said they had reviewed—as explicitly stating that recent warming was mostly man-made. Yet they stated, both in the paper itself and subsequently, that they had found a "97% consensus" explicitly stating that recent warming was mostly man-made.

Agnotology has the strong potential for misuse whereby a 'manufactured' consensus view can be used to stifle discussion, debate, and critical thinking.
                                                                    — Legates 2013

It appears that Cook and his co-authors manipulated the data to present an altogether untrue narrative of overwhelming support for catastrophic human-caused warming.

Note that the official "consensus" position—supported though it was by just 0.3% of the 11,944 papers reviewed—says nothing more than recent warming was mostly man-made. Even if that were the case—and the overwhelming majority of scientists take no view on that question, for it is beyond our present knowledge to answer—it would not indicate that global warming is dangerous.

If you tell a lie big enough and keep repeating it, people will eventually come to believe it.

— Joseph Goebbels

From the information we have just reviewed, the percentage of scientists who agree with the notion of man-made catastrophic global warming is significantly less than advertised. Several unbiased attempts have been made to assess what the actual number might be. One of the largest petitions concerning climate change was the Oregon Petition signed by more than 31,000 American scientists, including 9,029 holding PhDs, disputing the notion of anthropogenic climate alarmism (Figure II-1).

Figure II-1: The global warming petition that 31,000 scientists signed

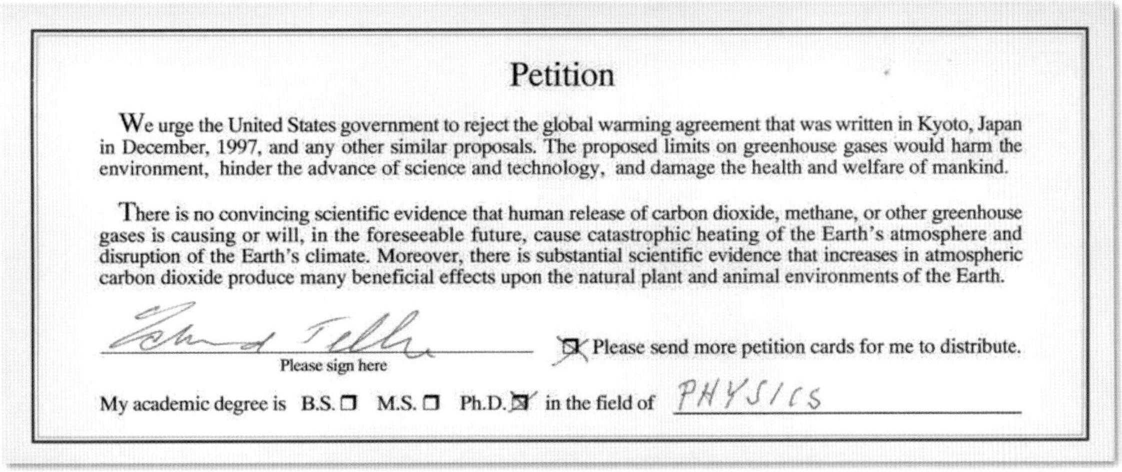

Petition

We urge the United States government to reject the global warming agreement that was written in Kyoto, Japan in December, 1997, and any other similar proposals. The proposed limits on greenhouse gases would harm the environment, hinder the advance of science and technology, and damage the health and welfare of mankind.

There is no convincing scientific evidence that human release of carbon dioxide, methane, or other greenhouse gases is causing or will, in the foreseeable future, cause catastrophic heating of the Earth's atmosphere and disruption of the Earth's climate. Moreover, there is substantial scientific evidence that increases in atmospheric carbon dioxide produce many beneficial effects upon the natural plant and animal environments of the Earth.

Please sign here

☒ Please send more petition cards for me to distribute.

My academic degree is B.S. ☐   M.S. ☐   Ph.D. ☒ in the field of *PHYSICS*

(Edward Teller's signature at http://petitionproject.com)

More recently, in 2016, George Mason University (Maibach 2016) surveyed more than 4,000 members of the American Meteorological Society and found that 33% believed that climate change was not occurring, was at most half man-made, was mostly natural, or they did not know. Significantly, only 18% believed that a large amount—or all—of additional climate change could be averted.

Inconvenient Fact 30

Only 0.3% of published scientists stated in their papers that recent warming was mostly man-made

Science does not advance through consensus, and the claim of consensus has no place in any rational scientific debate. We ask: What does the data tell us? What does it mean? Can we reproduce the results? If climate alarmists need to resort to an obviously flawed consensus opinion, rather than argue the merits of the science, haven't they already conceded that their argument cannot be won through open debate?

Inconvenient Fact 31

Science is not consensus and consensus is not science

Cook's 97% nonsensus [sic] paper shows that the climate community still has a long way to go in weeding out bad research and bad behavior. If you want to believe that climate researchers are incompetent, biased and secretive, Cook's paper is an excellent case in point.
— Professor Richard Tol

Let's be clear: the work of science has nothing whatever to do with consensus. Consensus is the business of politics. Science, on the contrary, requires only one investigator who happens to be right, which means that he or she has results that are verifiable by reference to the real world. In science consensus is irrelevant. What is relevant is reproducible results. The greatest scientists in history are great precisely because they broke with the consensus.

There is no such thing as consensus science. If it's consensus, it isn't science. If it's science, it isn't consensus. Period.
— Michael Crichton

Water, Water Everywhere — How Droughts are Declining

The impacts of climate change are expected to increase the frequency, intensity, and duration of droughts in many regions, and persistent drought could force foundational changes in the way communities use and live on the land.

> — The National Drought Resilience Partnership

Prolonged dry spells mean more than just scorched lawns. Drought conditions jeopardize access to clean drinking water, fuel out-of-control wildfires, and result in dust storms, extreme heat events, and flash flooding in the States.

> — Natural Resources Defense Council (NRDC)

One of the most-repeated hobgoblins of the global warming crowd is drought—a simple, understandable and frightening story, already familiar to hundreds of millions worldwide. According to the National Integrated Drought Information System, in the United States alone an eighth of the country and 80 million people were drought-stricken in early 2017 (Figure II-2).

Figure II-2: United States drought monitor

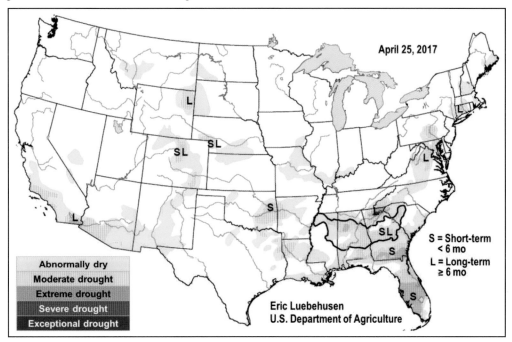

(National Integrated Drought Information System)

Within the United States, only hurricanes are costlier than droughts, and only then thanks to Hurricane Katrina (Ross and Lott 2003). Droughts have been and are easily demonized. They not only lead to local wildfires and water shortages, but also to wider effects on food and commodity prices. Are those who warn us of increasingly harmful effects of drought, like the NRDC, correct? Are these projections backed up with scientific evidence?

It is easy to persuade the public that global warming is causing droughts. After all, warmer temperatures should lead to drier conditions, then to drought. It seems obvious. Many climate scientists and government agencies have declared that droughts are becoming more frequent and more severe, owing to human-caused climate change.

Concerns were heightened by the intense drought that gripped the western United States from 1999 – 2016. As much as half of the contiguous United States saw moderate to severe drought and suffered from declines in water storage. It was a rare news report that failed to include a quote from a climatologist, blaming the dry conditions on human-induced climate change.

Once again, we have heard the predictions and conclusions of the climate "experts," but what does the data tell us?

Figure II-3 is a map showing the areas of the planet with increased vegetation density (greening) versus those areas which show vegetation loss (browning). This reveals that CO_2 fertilization and warming temperatures have been greening the Earth, rather than turning it to dust, as the prophets of doom tell us (de Jong 2011).

Figure II-3: Thanks to our changing climate, much of the world is greening.

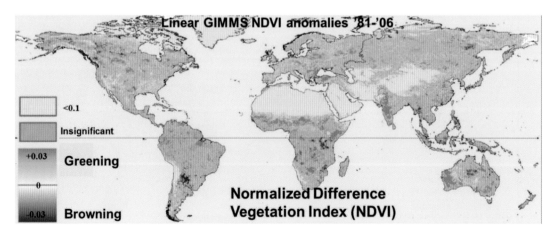

(Modified from de Jong 2011)

Two telling charts about drought are provided by government agencies. The first, from the EPA, shows the Palmer drought-severity index (Figure II-4). The second is a NOAA chart (2017a) of the areas of the United States over the last 120 years that indicate whether the year was wetter or dryer than average (Figure II-5). Both of these long-term data sets show absolutely nothing to indicate more frequent or more intense droughts.

Figure II-4: Palmer drought-severity index of mean drought conditions,
1895 – 2015

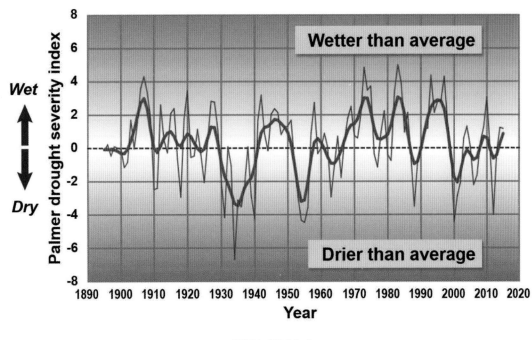

(EPA 2016a)

Figure II-6 shows the percentage of the world in various stages of drought. The data reveals that droughts across the world have been declining since the early 1980s.

A review of the most severe and persistent droughts of the 20th Century identified 30 of these severe droughts, including the Dust Bowl of the American Midwest in the 30s and the African Sahel drought of the 60s (Narisma 2007). Curiously, nearly 75% of the droughts occurred before 1960, and well before the bulk of the surge in atmospheric CO_2. According to this and other studies, rather than seeing a predicted increase in droughts, we are witnessing a significant decline in droughts, while both temperature and carbon dioxide increase (Fig. II-7).

Inconvenient Fact 32

More CO$_2$ ⇒ fewer droughts

Inconvenient Fact 33

Higher temperature ⇒ fewer droughts

Figure II-5: Percentage of United States very wet vs. very dry, 1895 – 2017

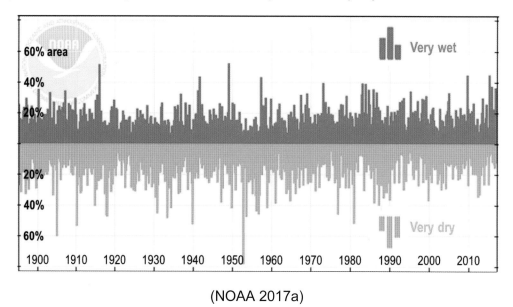

(NOAA 2017a)

Figure II-6: Percentage of the globe in drought, June 1983 to June 2012

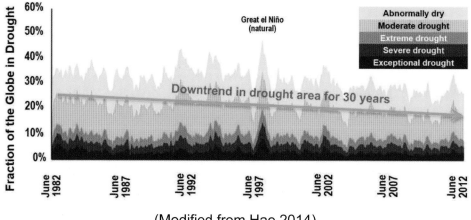

(Modified from Hao 2014)

Figure II-7: Global frequency of severe, persistent droughts, vs.
              temperature change and CO_2 emissions

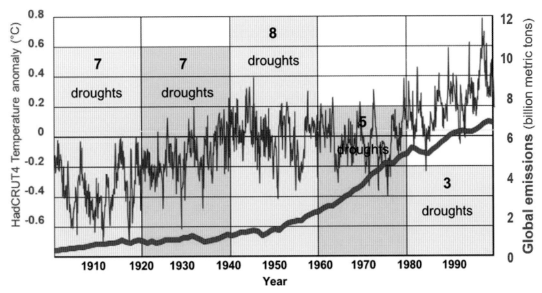

(Source data: drought: Narisma 2007, temperature: HadCrut4, CO_2: Boden 2016)

When we take a look at drought in the much longer term, that is, drought in the western United States going back more than 1,000 years, we find data that are very inconvenient to the official position of pending climate catastrophe (Cook 2007). The reconstructions from the study reveal the occurrence of past 'megadroughts' of unprecedented severity and duration (Figure II-8), ones that have never been experienced by modern societies in North America.

There is a scientific reason why one might expect fewer droughts. The dual effects of rising temperatures and increasing CO_2 are working together to increase the soil moisture around much of the world.

As we learned in the section on greenhouse warming, as the atmosphere warms, it is capable of carrying more water vapor. The additional water vapor tends to precipitate as rain. This increasing precipitation, owing to a warming world, is having its effect on once drought-stricken areas, such as the Sahel in the Western Sahara. The increased water vapor is directly leading to more rainfall, and huge increases in vegetation in formerly desert and semi-desert areas (Seaquist 2009). According to Martin Claussen of the Max Planck Institute, "The water-holding capacity of the air is the main driving force." It was reported that some 300,000 square kilometers of Saharan desert had become green over the previous 30 years, so much so that nomadic tribes were returning to places where they had not settled in living memory.

After visiting the Western Sahara in 2008, Stefan Kröpelin of the University of Cologne's Africa Research Unit stated: "Now you have people grazing their camels in areas which may not have been used for hundreds or even thousands of years. You see birds, ostriches, gazelles coming back, even sorts of amphibians coming back. The trend has continued for more than 20 years. It is indisputable (Owen 2009)."

Figure II-8: Long-term changes in aridity in western North America

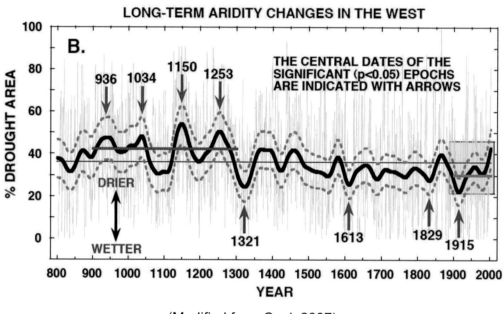

(Modified from Cook 2007)

You will recall from our section on CO_2, that increasing levels of the gas mean that plants' pores don't need to be open as long, reducing evaporation and increasing soil moisture. Increased resistance to drought because of soil moisture is a major benefit of increasing CO_2 concentrations. Inconvenient facts like these contradict the apocalyptic narrative of a world inexorably moving toward desertification.

The evidence is overwhelming: the only link between our changing climate and drought appears to be that there are *fewer* of these events, and they are *less intense*. This is an incredibly positive benefit for humankind and the ecosystems of the Earth. Yet the promoters of climate doom continue to assert just the opposite.

Forest Fires — Fanning the Flames of Needless Panic

The effects of global warming on temperature, precipitation levels, and soil moisture are turning many of our forests into kindling during wildfire season.

— Union of Concerned Scientists

No matter how hard we try, the fires are going to keep getting bigger, and the reason is really clear. We should be getting ready for bigger fire years than those familiar to previous generations.

— Park Williams, Columbia University researcher

Like many apocalyptic climate myths, there is wide acceptance among the media, "climate experts," and the general populace that forest fires are accelerating in frequency and size, owing to man-made climate change. As with drought, desertification, and heat waves, a link between warmer weather and more forest fires seems to be only common sense. Without specialist knowledge, one might logically surmise that warmer, and thus drier, weather means more fires.

The news media pumps up its ratings by broadcasting spectacular video footage and photographs of forest fires, particularly when they are fatal. During any large fire, the media proffers opinions of climate "experts" that man-made global warming is to blame for the loss of life and property.

So seldom is the truth revealed in the news media that many readers may well have assumed until now that supposed increasing frequency and ferocity of forest fires are caused by man-made global warming.

This is really a window into what global warming looks like. It looks like heat. It looks like dryness. It looks like this kind of disaster.

— Dr. Michael Oppenheimer

Many scientific studies forecast more forest fires on the basis of the same climate models that we have already seen to be fatally flawed in their predictive capabilities. Fortunately, we have data available to study the frequency of forest fires in both the recent and the distant past. The real-world data indicates that "experts" like Dr. Oppenheimer are, in fact, incredibly wrong on this subject.

We will look at the actual data that tells a story quite unlike the fake news peddled by the media and alarmist organizations. The National Interagency Fire Center provides extensive information on forest fires in the United States (NIFC 2017, Fig. II-9). The data clearly show a declining number of fires over the last 30 years. This mere fact is certainly at odds with everything we have heard to date on the subject.

Figure II-9: More CO_2, but fewer forest fires

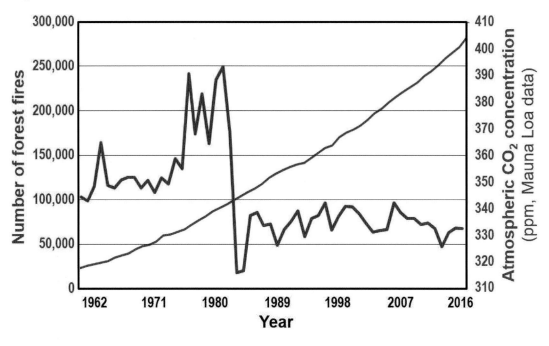

(Source data: Fires: NIFC 2017; CO_2: Tans 2017)

Inconvenient Fact 34

Forest fires across the northern hemisphere are decreasing.

A study by scientists with the Canadian Forest Service compared temperatures and CO_2 concentration versus frequency of forest fires over the last 150 years in North America and northern Europe (Flannigan 1998). Their results contradict the predictions of the promulgators of doom. The authors demonstrated a link between more CO_2 in the air and fewer fires worldwide. They attributed the decline in forest fires to the combined effect of CO_2 fertilization and rising temperature, leading to greater soil moisture. Their summary is worth reading:

> *Despite increasing temperatures since the end of the Little Ice Age (ca. 1850), wildfire frequency has decreased as shown by many field studies from North America and Europe. We believe that global warming since 1850 may have triggered decreases in fire frequency.*
> — Flannigan (1998)

A study in 2014 found that acreages burned worldwide in the 20th and early 21st centuries had declined significantly (Yang 2014, Figure II-10). The authors attributed the decline in high-latitude forest fires, particularly in most of North America and Europe, primarily to rising CO_2 concentrations. Just as was the case with declining trends in droughts, additional soil moisture, thanks to CO_2 fertilization, has probably been suppressing fires since significant amounts of CO_2 began being added to the atmosphere in the 20th Century.

Figure II-10: Global burned area by decade

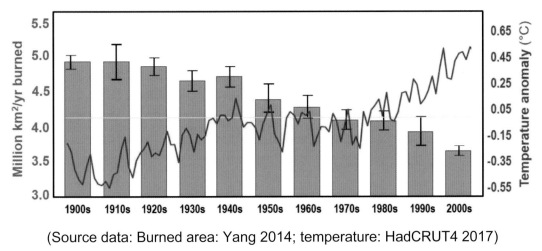

(Source data: Burned area: Yang 2014; temperature: HadCRUT4 2017)

The media and alarmist groups tell one story: the data tell quite another. Rather than an increase in the frequency and intensity of forest fires, as we have heard for many years, there are fewer forest fires, thanks to more CO_2 in the air and higher water vapor, linked to increasing temperatures. This is a very inconvenient fact for the anti-fossil-fuel groups that ruthlessly exploit the tragedies of others to raise funds for their causes. In the future, it will be very difficult to appeal for money on the basis of forest fires when it becomes known that *more CO_2 means fewer forest fires.*

Inconvenient Fact 35

More CO_2 » CO_2 fertilization » more soil moisture » faster tree growth » fewer forest fires

Famine: The Best Solution is More CO_2 and Increasing Temperature

In the long list of potential problems from global warming, the risks to world agriculture stand out as among the most important.
> — William R. Cline, Peterson Inst. for Int. Econ and Center for Global Development

Climate change is the biggest threat to our chances of winning the fight against hunger.
> — Winnie Byanyima, Executive Director of Oxfam International

A widely referenced paper in *The Lancet* predicted more than a half-million extra deaths by 2050, on account of famines caused by climate change. The author suggested that "climate change mitigation could prevent many climate-related deaths" and that negative dietary changes could "exceed other climate-related health impacts" (Springmann 2016). The implication is that, unless we embrace a low-carbon game plan now, we shall be directly responsible for deaths around the world. I certainly do not want to bear that burden. I'm sure you don't either. So let's take a look at the data.

Bear in mind that this prediction, and numerous other studies predicting famines, are based on exaggerated temperature models, and an assumed link to increasing droughts and heat waves that might cut food production. Yet, in the past, warmer weather has *always* meant *more* crops, while cooler times have led to famines and mass depopulations.

We shall see in this section that more CO_2 in the air and rising temperatures are already leading to plenty, not famine. By every important metric, global food production is growing—and growing not *in spite of* our changing climate but, in part, *because* of it. Warmer weather lengthens growing seasons and increases water vapor. CO_2 fertilization makes trees and plants more resistant to drought and fosters their growth, along with increasing the soil moisture around the world.

Inconvenient Fact 36

More CO_2 in the atmosphere means more food for everyone.

Take another look at Figure I-15 on Page 20. It shows that increasing CO_2 in the air to twice its pre-industrial concentration will benefit the 45 crops that constitute

95% of world food production. Based on this and hundreds of other research studies, we can expect CO_2 fertilization to boost food production significantly. The biomass of the top ten food crops would grow by more than a third if CO_2 concentration were to reach 600 parts per million. Idso (2013) has estimated that the CO_2-driven increase in the yield of the 45 crops in Figure I-15 in the 50 years 1961 – 2011 was worth $3 trillion.

Inconvenient Fact 37

The Earth is becoming greener, not turning into desert.

As we saw in Figure II-3, research has revealed that, over the last 25 years, the Earth has been *growing greener*, not turning into a desert (de Jong 2013). Confirmation of this comes from a recent study using satellite data from NASA showing increasing leaf cover over the last 35 years (Figure II-11). According to Zhu (2016) 25% to 50% of the Earth's surface has shown significant greening, while only 4% of the globe is browning. Importantly, the authors attribute the bulk of the greening to CO_2 fertilization effect.

Inconvenient Fact 38

Growing seasons are lengthening.

Warming temperatures are benefiting agricultural food production through lengthening growing seasons, which allow additional plantings (see Figure II-12). Killer frosts end earlier in the spring and arrive later in the autumn.

Inconvenient Fact 39

More CO_2 and warmer weather mean more world food production.

The world's remarkable ability to increase food production year after year is attributable to mechanization, agricultural innovation, CO_2 fertilization and warmer weather. World grain production and amount harvested per acre (Figures II-13 & II-14) show that crop and food production has steadily increased, with only positive effects from our changing climate.

Figure II-11: How green is my planet? CO_2 is making it greener.

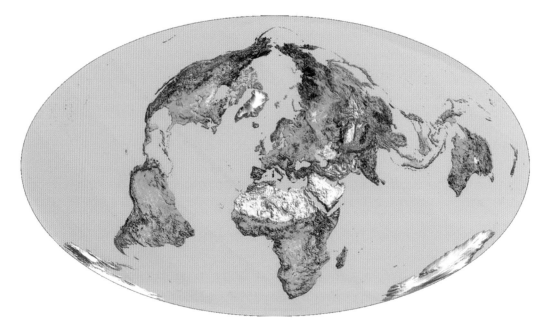

Change in leaf area, 1982-2015

< −30%   < −15%   −5%   +5%   +15%   +25%   +35%   > +50%

(Modified from NASA 2016, permission R Myneni)

Figure II-12: Trend in length of growing season (1981 – 2006)

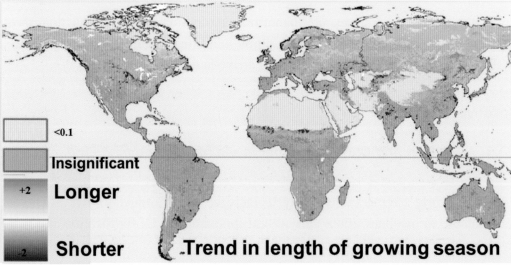

(Modified from de Jong 2011)

Figure II-13:   World grain production, CO₂ concentration and temperature, 1961 – 2014

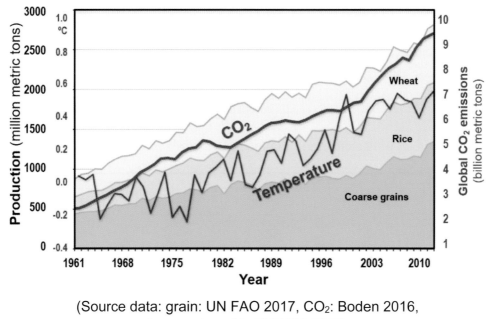

(Source data: grain: UN FAO 2017, CO₂: Boden 2016, temperature: HadCRUT4 2017)

Figure II-14:   Bushels of grain per acre harvested worldwide, 1936/37 – 2016/17

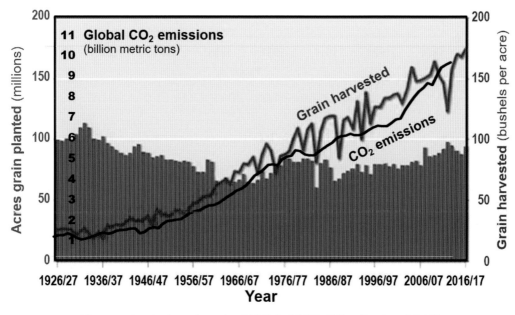

(Acres planted and grain: USDA 2017, CO₂: Boden 2016)

According to the USDA, corn is the largest component of the global grain trade, and the United States is the world's largest producer. Corn is thus one of the country's most important agricultural products, processed as sweet corn, cornmeal, tortillas, high-fructose corn syrup and, thankfully, bourbon. It also is the primary feedstock to fatten our cattle, chickens and hogs. Again, in Figure II-15, we see significant increases year after year, rather than the negative impacts predicted by the doom-mongers.

Figure II-15: CO_2 emissions go up, up goes U.S. corn production

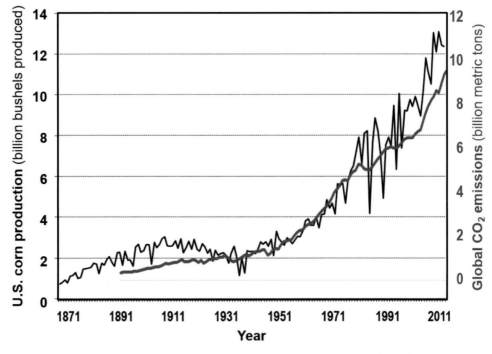

(Source data: Corn: UMiss 2011; CO_2: Boden 2016)

Corn production in the U.S. presents a conundrum for environmental activists. On the one hand, there is significant fear-mongering over predicted declines in food productivity based on questionable climate models. On the other hand, the enemies of fossil fuels promote ethanol production to replace our oil-based transportation fuels. Every acre of corn diverted to ethanol production is an acre that is no longer feeding the world's hungry. In 2008, Herr Jean Ziegler, the United Nations' Rapporteur for the Right to Food, claimed that "to divert land from food production to biofuels is a crime against humanity."

The share of corn production devoted to ethanol production in the U.S. has skyrocketed from just a few percent in the late 1990s to 39% recently. Meanwhile, the government mandated that 42% of the crop be dedicated to ethanol in 2016. Driven by unneeded environmentalist demands, the U.S. is increasingly moving toward fueling its cars with a food product at the expense of nutrition for the world's poorest.

Figure II-16: U.S. corn feeds cars, not people, 1980/81 – 2016/17

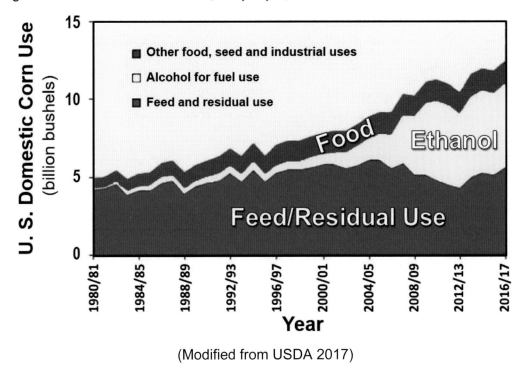

(Modified from USDA 2017)

Summary — Food Abundance

If more CO$_2$ and warmer weather were going to cause a decline in world-wide food production, should there not have been some recognizable negative effects by now, after 150 years? Contrary to predictions, all the signs point to robust food production, which will increase far into the foreseeable future. We can be grateful for a combination of rising temperatures and increasing carbon dioxide—unless, that is, we return to the low temperatures of the Little Ice Age.

Heat and Life, Cold and Death

Heat waves could be an average of 10°F hotter by the end of the century.
— Natural Resources Defense Council (NRDC) 2017

Global warming is bringing more frequent and severe heat waves, and the result will be serious for vulnerable populations. That means air pollution in urban areas could get worse, bringing increased risk of heart attacks, strokes and asthma attacks. Children, the elderly, poor, and people of color are especially vulnerable to these effects.
— Dr. Amanda Staudt, National Wildlife Federation climate scientist

The assessment that man-made global warming will lead to massive increases in heat waves and heat-related deaths is stated as fact by every governmental climate agency and group promoting a link between increasing CO_2 and the warming of the last century. The National Climate Assessment (2014) said, "The number of heat waves has been increasing in recent years." The reliably unreliable U.S. Global Change Research Program makes the following assertions (USGCRP 2009):

Increases in morbidity and mortality from extreme heat are very likely;

Temperatures are rising and the probability of severe heat waves is increasing;

Rare and extreme heat waves will become much more common;

Heat is already the leading cause of weather-related deaths in the United States.

Are these assertions correct? What does the science tell us? In this chapter, we shall review the historical records and the inconvenient scientific facts about extreme heat waves, giving you enough data to make a reasonable judgment for yourself.

Inconvenient Fact 40

EPA: Heat waves are not becoming more frequent.

We shall start with the EPA's own data (2016b) which show no increase in heat waves in recent years. Instead, there was a remarkable spike in extreme heat waves in the 1930s, long before we could have affected the climate to any significant degree (Figure II-17).

Figure II-17: Nature, not CO_2 emissions, drives heat waves

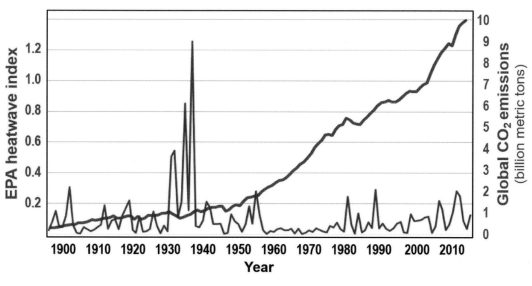

(Heatwave: EPA 2016b, CO_2: Boden 2016)

John Christy of the University of Alabama at Huntsville is the State Climatologist and provides useful charts of high temperatures (Christy 2015). Figure II-18 shows the percentage of days that exceeded 100°F at almost 1,000 NOAA stations across the United States. Note that the lower 48 states of the U.S. have seen an 80-year decline in extreme heat.

Inconvenient Fact 41

Extreme heat events are declining.

There has been a distinct, long-term decrease from the excessively hot temperatures of the 1930s. Figure II-19, a summary of 130 years of daily maximum summer temperatures in Alabama, confirms a decline in extreme heat waves in the southeastern U.S. since the 19th Century.

Inconvenient Fact 42

Cold kills far more people than heat every year.

Climate extremists predict that heat waves and high temperatures related to global warming will kill increasingly more people worldwide. As usual, the inconvenient facts are otherwise. If the merchants of doom were right, the warming over the last 150 years should have been reflected in more deaths caused by heat waves.

Figure II-18: Up goes CO₂ concentration, down go heat waves

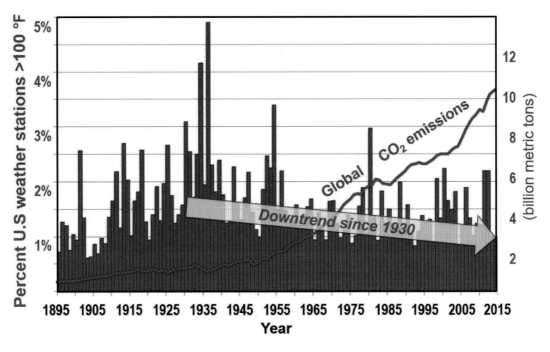

(Heat: Modified from Christy 2015, Source CO₂: Boden 2016)

Figure II-19: In Alabama, peak daily temperature fell from 1883 – 2014.

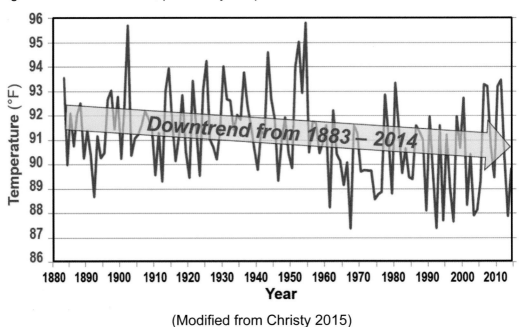

(Modified from Christy 2015)

The inconvenient fact is that cold kills considerably more people than heat. It is, by far, the biggest weather-related killer worldwide. Warmer weather would mean far fewer premature temperature-related deaths.

A study of temperature-associated mortality in the U.K. and Australia found that cold-related deaths in the U.K. and Australia accounted for 61 and 33 deaths per million, respectively, while heat-related deaths were only three and two per million (Vardoulakis 2014). *Cold kills more than 15 times as many people in these countries as heat.*

In the largest study to date on deaths attributable to heat or cold, Gasparrini (2015) and a large team of collaborators from around the world examined more than 74 million deaths in 13 countries between 1985 and 2012. Warm countries included Thailand and Brazil; temperate countries included Australia; cold countries included Sweden. The aim was to determine the number of deaths attributable to either heat or cold.

The study revealed that *cold weather kills 20 times as many people as heat.* Worse, one in 15 deaths, from all causes, was attributable to cold. Only one death in 250 was attributable to heat. In every country examined, cold-related deaths greatly outnumbered deaths from heat (Fig. II-20).

Figure II-20: Cold weather, not hot weather, is the real killer.

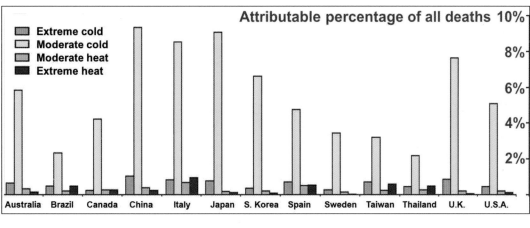

(Gasparrini 2015)

Note that, in Figure II-20, by far the largest number of temperature-related deaths comes from moderate cold. Of course, moderate cold occurs far more frequently than extreme cold: but these figures show, and show clearly, that even a modest *decrease* in temperature is more likely to kill, while even a large increase is not.

Inconvenient Fact 43

Warmer weather means many fewer temperature-related deaths.

Inconvenient Fact 44

Warmer weather prevents millions of premature deaths each year.

In the United States, summer heat-related deaths have declined dramatically (Fig. II-21) in the last half of the 20th century (Kalkstein 2011 and Davis 2003).

Figure II-21: Warmer weather, yet fewer deaths from warmer weather

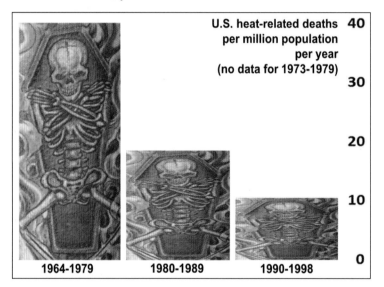

(Kalkstein 2011 and Davis 2003; modified from Michaels 2012)

Between 1979 and 2006, United States annual death rates from heat declined by 10%, while deaths from cold fell by a dramatic 37% (Goklany 2009). In fact, extreme-weather deaths and death rates have been tumbling since the 1920s, notwithstanding the modest global warming since then (Figure II-22).

"Excess winter mortality" is the statisticians' description of premature deaths from cold. The British Office for National Statistics studied such deaths for recent winters in England and Wales and found that 24,300 excess winter deaths had occurred during the winter of 2015 – 16. Importantly, the British statisticians found a strong and persistent decline in excess winter mortality over the past 60 years. Only half as many die before their time in winter today as did in the 1950s (Fig. II-23).

People are dying of cold in Britain today not so much because the weather is cold as because their homes are cold. Following a "green"-driven tripling of energy prices over the past two decades, in order to subsidize otherwise uneconomic windmills, many of those who died did so because they could no longer afford to heat their homes. It is safe to say that far more people have died worldwide as a result of no doubt well-intentioned, but misguided, "save-the-planet" policies, than have died as a result of modest global warming.

A study by the European Union predicts that a future reduction in deaths from cold will significantly outweigh any increase in deaths from heat by the year 2080 (Ciscar 2009). By that year, the author predicts, 162,000 additional premature deaths per year from heat will be outweighed by the predicted 256,000 deaths per year from cold that would be prevented (Fig. II-24). In Europe alone, the study predicts that *close to 100,000 people a year would be spared an untimely death—thanks to global warming.* That being the case, we should all welcome the increasing warmth that will lengthen the global average life span.

Disingenuous statements such as those issued from the U.S. Global Change Research Program that increased mortality from extreme heat was "very likely," and that "some reduction in the risk of death related to extreme cold is expected." The statistics tell us that temperature-related deaths are decreasing around the world and that the decline in cold-linked mortality is particularly dramatic. And that—except in the world of climate extremism—is a very good thing.

Figure II-22: U.S. annual extreme-weather deaths and death rates tumble.

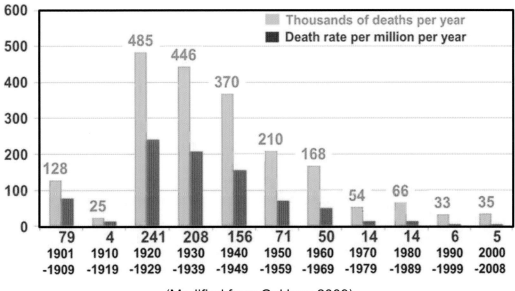

(Modified from Goklany 2009)

Figure II-23: Good news—cold is killing fewer Britons

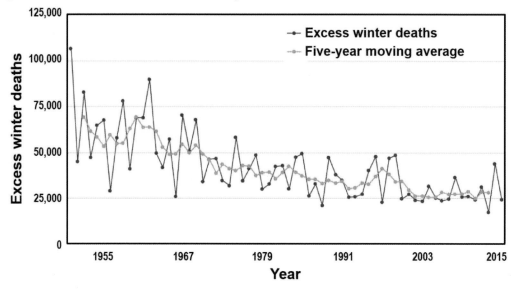

(U.K. Office for National Statistics 2017)

Figure II-24: The more the global warming, the fewer the predicted deaths
from temperature

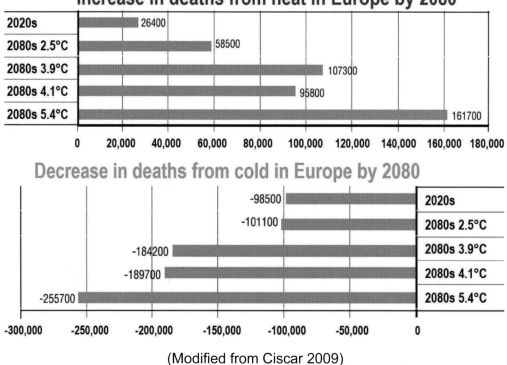

(Modified from Ciscar 2009)

Inconvenient Fact 45

More CO₂ and warmth mean shorter, less intense heat waves.

We have seen in the chapters on food shortages, forest fires, and drought, that the combination of higher CO_2 concentration and warmer weather is boosting soil moisture worldwide, because of increased water vapor and the CO_2 fertilization of plants. Studies of European heat waves from 1970 – 2000 (Fischer 2007a), and especially of the devastating European heat wave of 2003 (Fischer 2007b), found that decreased soil moisture was the primary cause. They estimated that the warming might have been 40% less with normal soil moisture. The conclusion: if the soil had not been unusually dry, "summer 2003 would still have been warm, but it would not have been such a devastating event as it turned out to be."

Figure II-25: As temperature dropped, U.K. deaths increased—and vice versa.

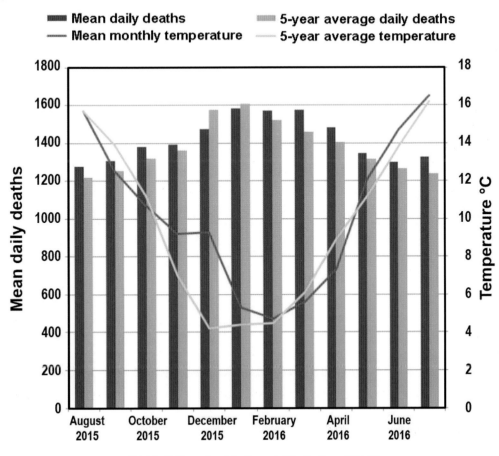

(U.K. Office for National Statistics 2017)

Summary — A Warm Climate Is Good for Us

The facts starkly challenge the contention that warmer weather kills. The truth is that warmer weather has already cut temperature-related deaths, and will continue to do so, directly raising life expectancies around the world. The facts and the data demonstrate exactly the opposite of what the prognosticators of climate doom predict. If this important element of the alarmist campaign is so easily debunked by so many scientific studies, shouldn't one also look with a critical eye at all the other hobgoblins of alarm?

In a Whirl About Tornadoes

The recent trend of severe and lethal tornadoes are (sic) part of a global trend toward more storms.
> — Paul Epstein, in *The Atlantic,* July 8, 2011

It is irresponsible not to mention climate change in the context of these extreme tornadoes.
> — Dr. Kevin Trenberth, US National Center for Atmospheric Research

The amount of tornadoes…it's like three times the highest amount ever before, right? Something weird is happening with all of these natural catastrophes.
> — Rosie O'Donnell on Rosie Radio, May 26, 2011

Tornadoes are particularly feared in the United States because they kill and injure more U.S. citizens than any other type of storm. While many other countries are spared the twisters' wrath, the United States is the world leader in the number of tornadoes per year—1,250—with Canada trailing in a distant second place, with just 100. Other countries, most of them in mid-latitudes, have tornadoes as well (Fig. II-26).

Figure II-26: Tornadoes world distribution

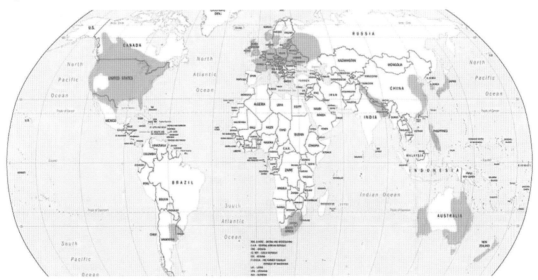

(NOAA 2017a)

The unique geography of the U.S. makes it tornado-prone. The Rocky Mountains and the Gulf of Mexico provide the key ingredients for formation of the severe thunderstorms that spawn tornadoes: warm, moist air close to the ground; cool, dry air aloft; and horizontal winds that travel faster aloft than near the surface.

NOAA (2017b) says early historic records of tornadoes are unreliable: "One of the main difficulties with tornado records is that a tornado, or evidence of a tornado, must have been observed. Unlike rainfall or temperature, which may be measured by a fixed instrument, tornadoes are short-lived and very unpredictable. A tornado in a largely unoccupied region is not likely to be documented. Many significant tornadoes may not have made it into the historical record, since Tornado Alley was very sparsely populated during the early 20th Century."

With increasing population, Doppler radar detection and better reporting, the number of tornadoes identified has significantly increased in recent years. Because of this, NOAA recommends only using the strongest tornadoes as a measure of pre-radar numbers. Large and violent tornadoes might well have been identified even in days before better reporting was in place. Figure II-30 shows a tornado's rank.

Inconvenient Fact 46

The number of tornadoes is decreasing.

Inconvenient Fact 47

The number of tornadoes in 2016 was the lowest on record.

The chart below of these very strong tornadoes ($\geq$F 3.0) shows declining numbers of tornadoes over the last 60 years (Fig. II-27).

The year 2016 ended with the lowest tornado count that NOAA (2016) has ever recorded (Figure II-28). How can that be? Isn't climate change supposed to be increasing these storms? The answer—not that you will hear it in the biased news media—is No. Outside the tropics (and probably within the tropics, too), storminess of all kinds is expected to decrease gently with warmer weather, because it is differentials between temperatures that cause storms, and warming reduces those differentials.

Greater improvements in detection and early warning are the primary reason that deaths per million due to tornadoes in the U.S. have been in a long-term decline (Figure II-29), but a decline in the number of the storms surely cannot hurt.

Figure II-27: Severe tornadoes (F 3+) are less frequent than 50 years ago.

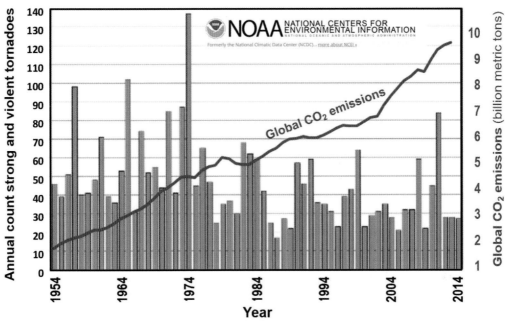

(Tornadoes NOAA 2017b, CO₂: Boden 2016)

Figure II-28: 2016—Lowest number of tornadoes according to NOAA

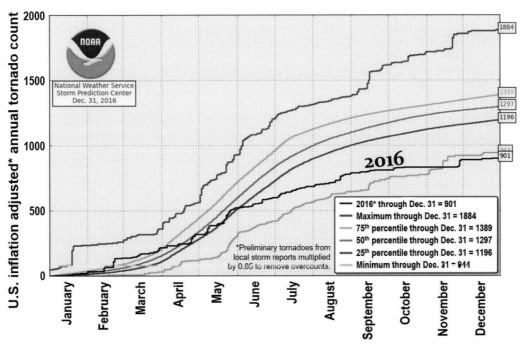

(NOAA 2016)

Figure II-29: U.S. tornado deaths per million population

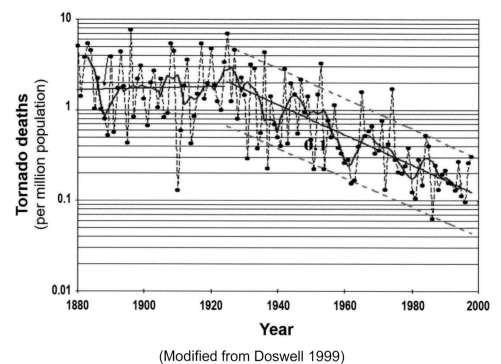

(Modified from Doswell 1999)

Inconvenient Fact 48

Deaths from tornadoes are falling.

That the science, the facts and the data show absolutely no correlation between tornadoes and rising temperatures over the last half-century and more has not stopped climate extremists from linking nearly every tornado catastrophe to global warming. Rosie O'Donnell, hardly a scientist, can be forgiven for making uninformed comments linking tornadoes to climate change. The scientific community has no such excuse.

Figure II-30: The Fujita tornado scale

F	0	1	2	3	4	5
Fastest ¼ mile (mph)	40 – 72	73 – 112	113 – 157	158 – 207	208 – 260	261 – 318
Fastest 3-second gust (mph)	45 – 78	79 – 117	118 – 161	162 – 209	210 – 261	262 – 318

(NOAA 2017c)

Hurricanes — Politicizing Tragedy

The hurricane that struck Louisiana yesterday was nicknamed Katrina by the National Weather Service. Its real name is global warming.
— Ross Gelbspan, *Boston Globe* op-ed,
August 30, 2005

It's not a pretty picture, hurricanes could become more intense as the Earth warms. They are frightening, destructive and extremely costly, and we expect future hurricanes to leave an even greater trail of damage in their wake.
— Michael Oppenheimer, Professor of
Geosciences, Princeton University

The intensity, frequency, and duration of North Atlantic hurricanes, as well as the frequency of the strongest hurricanes, have all increased since the early 1980s. Hurricane intensity and rainfall are projected to increase as the climate continues to warm.
— National Climate Assessment, 2014

Alarmists have been predicting an increase in the frequency, intensity and duration of hurricanes since they first started linking humankind's CO_2 emissions to global warming. We are guaranteed that every hurricane or tropical depression that makes landfall will be accompanied by extensive media coverage, with claims of a link between the latest storm tragedies and global warming. The theory behind the connection between warming and hurricane activity is superficially plausible. Global warming raises ocean surface temperatures, fueling tropical cyclones and hurricanes. That seems to be a perfectly reasonable prediction. Yet the facts say otherwise.

Promoters of the notion that warming worsens hurricanes, including the authors of the *National Climate Assessment* of 2014, often refer to a chart (Figure II-31) of the North Atlantic hurricane power-dissipation index. This index is an aggregate of factors that measure total hurricane power over a hurricane season. They concluded that there was a "strong upward trend" in the Atlantic region. But they were not telling the whole story.

Patrick Michaels points out in his book, *Lukewarming* (2015), how odd it was that the dataset only began in 1970 and, still more curiously, ended in 2009. This was despite the fact there was long-term data available before 1970, and four additional seasons with no land-falling storms after 2009. Michaels provides a longer-term evaluation of the power-dissipation index from Dr. Ryan Maue, this time showing the full dataset, including the recent years with no land-falling Atlantic hurricanes. The "upward trend" of the *Climate Assessment* was, in reality, no uptrend at all (Fig. II-32).

Michaels concluded: "Datasets should be viewed in their entirety, not cherry-picked."

To make things even more inconvenient for the alarmists, the authors of the study which provided the data for Figure II-31 wrote: "We were not able to corroborate the presence of upward trends in hurricane intensity over the past two decades in any basin other than the Atlantic. Since the Atlantic basin accounts for less than 15% of global hurricane activity, this result poses a challenge to hypotheses that directly relate globally increasing tropical SST (surface sea temperature) to increases in long-term mean global hurricane intensity" (Kossin 2007).

The authors of the *National Climate Assessment* not only used cherry-picked data: they misstated the conclusions reached by the authors of the dataset.

Inconvenient Fact 49

There has been no increase in frequency of hurricanes in recent data.

Figure II-31: Cherry-picked trends in North Atlantic hurricane power

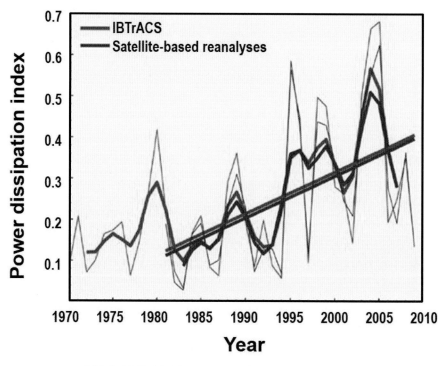

(USGCRP 2014, adapted from Kossin 2007)

Figure II-32: The true long-term trend in North Atlantic hurricanes PDI

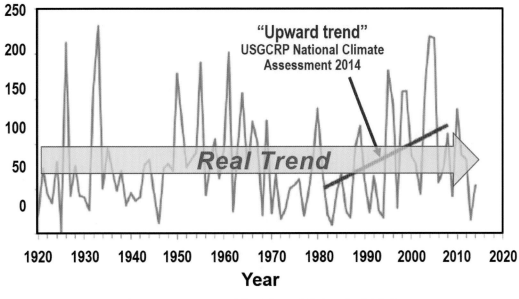

(Maue 2016, modified from Michaels 2015)

Below are two charts showing global hurricane and tropical storm data compiled by Dr. Ryan Maue (Figures II-33 and II-34). The charts show no rising trend. In fact, a compelling argument could be made for a decline over the last 30 years or more.

Figure II-33: Frequency of global hurricanes and major hurricanes

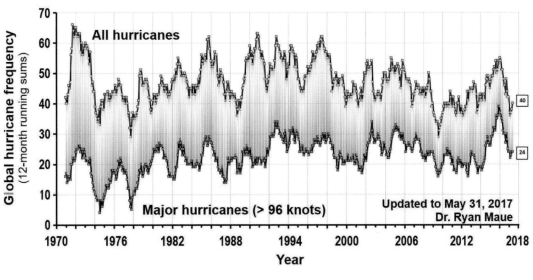

(Maue 2017)

Figure II-34: Global tropical storm and hurricane frequency is falling.

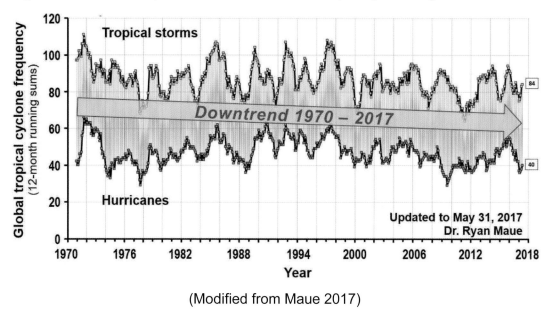

(Modified from Maue 2017)

Inconvenient Fact 50

We have seen 250 years of declining hurricane frequency.

As further confirmation that there is no upward trend in hurricane frequency, intensity or duration, researchers at the National University of Mexico reviewed data going back to the year 1749 and found that "from 1749 to 2012 the linear trend in the number of hurricanes is decreasing" (Rojo-Garibaldi 2016, Figure II-35).

So what are promoters of warm-ology to do when they just can't get the data to cooperate with their preconceived notions? The answer is to fund more studies. In this case, researchers from Florida State conducted a study that used complex climate models (recall how well those have worked out) to predict that hurricanes will become fewer but more intense (Kang 2015). Climate Armageddon proponents have latched onto this idea of "fewer but bigger" storms to continue to promote fear.

Christopher Landsea, a meteorologist for the National Hurricane Center, has quantified what an increase in the intensity of major hurricanes, driven by global-warming, may mean (Landsea 2011). His work indicates that the warming over the last several decades translates into an increase in intensity of about 1%. For a Category 5 hurricane like Katrina, the wind speed would increase by 1 to 2 mph. He wrote: "The 1-2 mph change currently in the peak winds of strong hurricanes due to manmade global warming is so tiny that it is not measurable by our aircraft and satellite technologies available today, which are only accurate to about 10 mph (~15 kph) for major hurricanes."

In other words, the estimated increase in hurricane strength is too small to be significant.

Inconvenient Fact 51

No significant increase in hurricane intensity due to warming

Figure II-35: Hurricane frequency fell for more than 250 years.

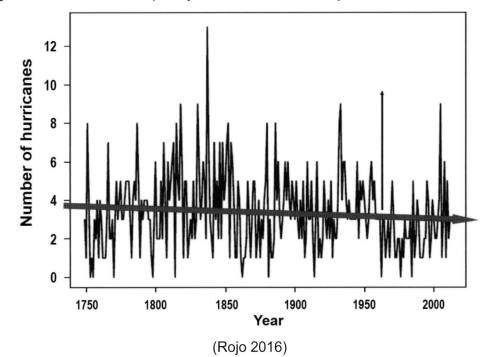

(Rojo 2016)

Polar Bears are Doing Just Fine, Thank You

Climate change is drowning and starving polar bears. If greenhouse gas-fueled climate change keeps melting their sea-ice habitat, an Arctic apocalypse will wipe them out in a century—and they'll disappear from the United States by 2050.

— Center for Biological Diversity

Our analyses highlight the potential for large reductions in the global polar-bear population if sea-ice loss continues, which is forecast by climate models and other studies

— IPCC (2013)

In May 2008, the U.S. Fish and Wildlife Service listed the polar bear, *Ursus maritimus*, as a threatened species under the Endangered Species Act, predicting that bear populations would decline by two-thirds as the sea ice they rely on for hunting continued to shrink. This conclusion was not based on evidence that the numbers of these iconic animals were declining—the opposite was the case—but they were put on the list based on predicted future dangers, using the flawed climate models discussed in previous chapters.

The Fish and Wildlife Service's thesis is that:

– sea ice is shrinking because of global warming.

– polar bears need sea ice to hunt seals.

– cuddly polar bears will starve or drown unless we change our evil ways.

Patrick Michaels, the Cato Institute's senior fellow, disputed the science behind the decision, saying, "This marks the first instance of a species being listed based upon a computer model of future climate."

Again, we will look at the science, the facts and data, to get to the truth regarding our great, white, furry friends. As we shall see, the data are entirely inconvenient for environmentalist groups trying to raise donations on the pretext that polar bears are on the brink of extinction.

Far from becoming extinct polar bear populations are doing well, in fact:

Polar-bear populations are increasing;

Polar bears in regions with the greatest ice loss are thriving;

Polar bears survived a previous much warmer period.

It is difficult and dangerous to assess the population of polar bears accurately. Their home turf is mostly barren, snowy, windswept terrain that is inhospitable to humans, whose census-taking bears do not welcome. Also, humans apparently taste a lot like seal, or enough so that we are on the bear menu.

Despite these challenges, the most recent population studies actually indicate that polar bear populations are rising fast and are *at a 50-year high* (Fig. II-36). A recent report by Susan Crockford, a noted polar bear expert, reveals that the current population of 22,000 to 31,000 is the highest estimate in more than 50 years.

Figure II-36: There are almost four times as many polar bears as in 1960.

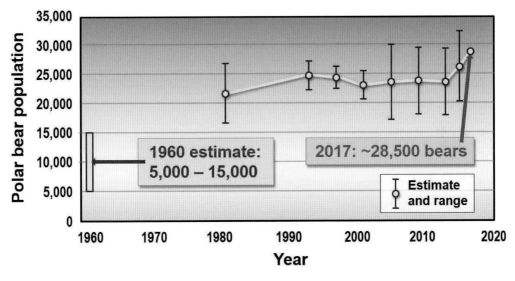

(Modified from Crockford 2015)

Inconvenient Fact 52

> *The population of polar bears is growing.*

Inconvenient Fact 53

> *There are more polar bears now than we've had for 50 years.*

A recent review of Canadian polar bears found stable or increasing numbers in 12 of 13 sub-populations (York 2016, Figure II-37). The researchers concluded: "We do not find support for the perspective that polar bears within or shared with Canada are currently in any sort of climate crisis." That is quite a bit different than anything you have likely read or heard about concerning this issue.

Figure II-37: Twelve of 13 regional polar bear populations are thriving.

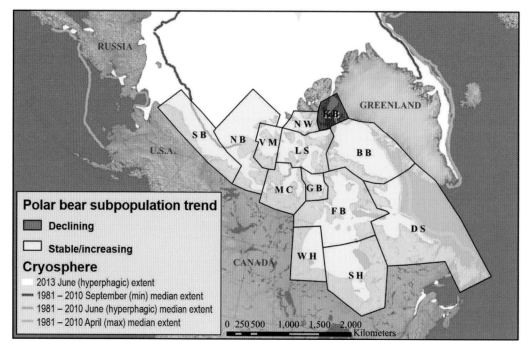

(York 2016)

Inconvenient Fact 54

Polar bears are thriving even where sea ice is diminishing.

Extraordinarily inconvenient recent results of polar bear research do not support the narrative that decreasing sea ice is detrimental to the bears' health (Rode 2014). In fact, they appear to be quite fat and happy in areas of high ice loss. Rode's study compared bears in the Chukchi and Beaufort Seas, bounding Alaska and Russia (Fig. II-38). The Chukchi Sea had lost twice as much ice as the Beaufort Sea. The researchers had expected that the Chukchi Sea bears would have suffered, yet they found just the opposite.

By every metric, the authors found that bears in the region that had the most ice loss were healthier and fatter than in the area with less ice loss. The females were heavier by almost 70 pounds (30 kg), and males by 110 pounds (50 kg). See Figure II-39, below.

Chukchi sows had larger litters with higher survival rates, and yearlings' weight exceeded their counterparts in the Beaufort Sea by nearly 50 pounds (25 kg). The researchers concluded that less ice led to "higher ecosystem productivity," that is, more critters to eat.

Amusingly, the researchers—having not found the result that they, or their funding sources had expected—ended their report by wondering about the difficulty of "messaging this complexity to the public."

We didn't have to wait very long to see how this combination of less ice and healthier bears would be conveyed by the promoters of climate doom to the public: A June 2017 study by the USGS and the University of Wyoming (Durner 2017) concluded that bears in areas of high ice loss would need to consume more calories through increased foraging and would need to kill 2% to 6% more seals to make up for it.

Figure II-38: Polar bears are thriving in high ice-loss areas.

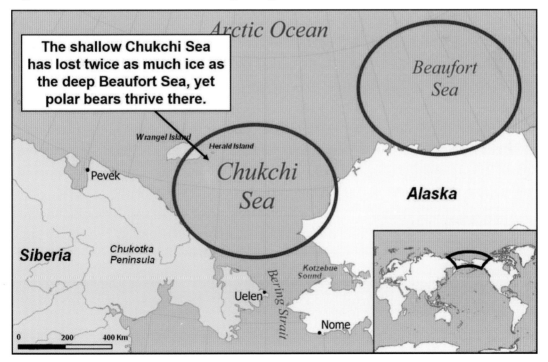

(Map adapted from Wikimaps)

Figure II-39: Male polar bear weight comparison of the two populations

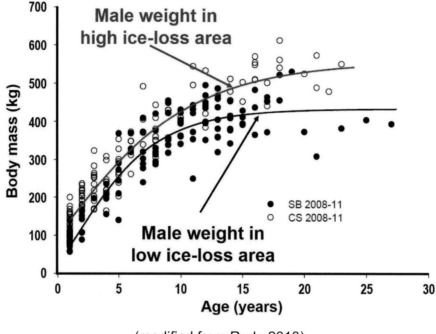

(modified from Rode 2013)

AP's reporting on this latest study confirmed that man's consumption of fossil fuels almost certainly will lead to the bears' extinction. Not until 800 words into the AP story, near the end, do we get this hidden gem: "Bears in the Chukchi Sea, off Alaska's northwest coast, had to walk farther and burn more calories than south Beaufort bears *but are in better shape because more food is available.*"

So it appears that the "simple bear necessities" *may not actually include ice.*

Indeed, it will be a lot harder to raise money for the World Wildlife Fund once it gets out that warmer temperatures mean more polar bears. The bears, after all, originated on land and migrated to the ice about 150,000 years ago. Like us, they are warm-blooded creatures. Like us, they prefer warmer to colder weather.

Finally, we have seen from the chapter on temperatures that several climate *optima* (that is, warming periods) in our current interglacial period had much higher temperatures than we enjoy today, and there was probably a lot less polar sea ice then than now. In fact, the last interglacial period, more than 120,000 years ago, was 8°C (14°F) warmer than today, with no polar ice at all (Dahl-Jensen 2013). Yet the polar bear survived.

The bears will survive in our own time, too, as long as hunting—the only real threat to them—is carefully controlled. So rest easy, polar bear enthusiasts, your great, white friends will do quite nicely in a warming world.

Ocean Acidity — Climate pHraud

*Ocean life dependent on carbonate shells and skeletons is threatened by
dissolution as the ocean becomes more acid.*
> — James Hansen, Director of the Program on Climate
> Science, Columbia University Earth Institute

Ocean acidification is climate change's equally evil twin.
> — Jane Lubchenco, former Head of NOAA

Ocean "acidification," the latest climate hobgoblin to be advanced as a result of increasing CO_2 levels, began to be heavily promoted as the "evil twin" of global warming when it became clear that the 25-year warming trend of the late 20th Century had ended, and a long pause in temperature increase had begun. Ocean "acidification" became the fallback pretext for the anti-fossil-fuel agenda, just in case its specter of a sizzling Earth collapsed under the weight of evidence against it.

This chapter is somewhat more technical than the others, but the detail is necessary if you are to see why the climate extremists are just as wrong on ocean chemistry as they are on atmospheric physics.

Before 2004, very little attention had been focused on ocean "acidification," but that all changed quite suddenly. Howard Browman of the Institute of Marine Research did a thorough study and found that, though there had been no learned papers on the subject before, from 2006 to 2015 more than 3,100 papers had appeared (Figure II-40). He called the explosion of research on the topic "unprecedented in marine sciences" and reported that nearly all published articles predicted an "acidification" calamity, while studies that found no link were difficult to publish. There is no surprise here: "fund it and they will find it."

So what is ocean "acidification?" Here is a quick refresher on acidity, alkalinity and pH. The measurement of acidity or alkalinity, known as pH (that is, the proportion of hydrogen ions compared with distilled water), ranges from very acidic (pH 0), such as battery acid, to very alkaline (pH 14), such as lye or drain cleaner (Fig. II-41). Neutral is pH 7.0. Rainwater is quite acidic, at pH 5.4, while seawater is pronouncedly alkaline, at pH 7.8 to 8.1.

Alarm over ocean "acidification" is based on the theory that elevated atmospheric CO_2 causes more CO_2 to be dissolved into the ocean, increasing the concentration of carbonic acid, particularly near the surface, and making it impossible for shelled invertebrates (such as crabs or corals) to create the calcium carbonate that makes up their shells and exoskeletons. A further lowering of pH (increasing acidity),

Figure II-40: Academia on acid: papers about the "acid" ocean, 2001 – 2015

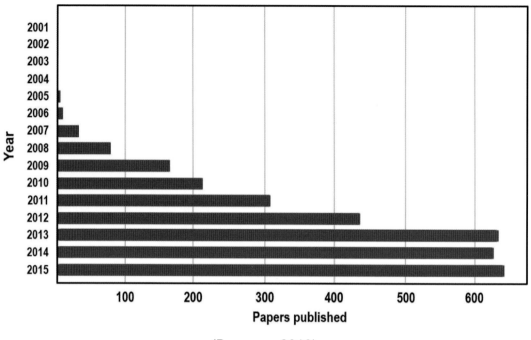

(Browman 2016)

so the extremists say, would begin dissolving the shells of existing creatures, resulting in an oceanic apocalypse.

The "calcifying organisms"—creatures that make their shells or exoskeletons out of calcium carbonate—already are used to very large swings in pH on the continental shelves near the mouths of rivers, particularly during floods. The rivers that flow into the bays and estuaries are often significantly acidified, yet oyster communities thrive in those areas. In fact, the federal government acknowledges this with a lower allowable limit of 6.5 (that's acid) for the Clean Water Act. For example, the wonderfully delicious oysters from the Chesapeake Bay of the eastern U.S. do quite nicely in a bay that commonly approaches 7.0 due to river influx, far lower than the most radical predictions of the alarmists.

Have our oceans been acidic before? Our very earliest oceans, more than 2 billion years ago, are thought to have been acidic (Halevy 2017). However, since those earliest oceans, the only time that the ocean was actually acidic was about 54 million years ago (Zachos 2005). The cause for that period of acid oceans was attributed by Zachos to a sudden release of methane, rather than an increase in CO_2 (CO_2 levels were ~850 ppm at that time, much less than the 2,600 ppm average for the Earth's last 650 million years).

Figure II-41: pH values of common substances

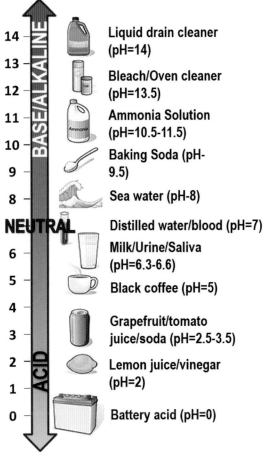

14	Liquid drain cleaner (pH=14)
13	
12	Bleach/Oven cleaner (pH=13.5)
11	Ammonia Solution (pH=10.5-11.5)
10	
9	Baking Soda (pH-9.5)
8	Sea water (pH-8)
NEUTRAL	Distilled water/blood (pH=7)
6	Milk/Urine/Saliva (pH=6.3-6.6)
5	Black coffee (pH=5)
4	
3	Grapefruit/tomato juice/soda (pH=2.5-3.5)
2	Lemon juice/vinegar (pH=2)
1	
0	Battery acid (pH=0)

The pH of the ocean varies slightly, depending on season, water depth and latitude. The pH level trends slightly less alkaline in the tropics, during the winter, and at depth. According to many estimates, the oceans' pH has declined slightly (~0.1 pH) since the beginning of the Industrial Revolution.

IPCC models predict that ocean alkalinity may decline another 0.3 pH by the year 2100. Although this level is unlikely to be reached, even if it were true, the ocean would remain firmly alkaline. In fact, since the current range of estimates of ocean alkalinity is pH 7.8 – 8.1, the small change predicted by the alarmists is barely beyond the estimates of alkalinity today. They dare not predict large changes; instead, they pretend that the small changes they predict will have large effects.

The prediction of increasing acidity and the doom of the sea is based almost entirely on models that use the following reasoning:

More CO_2 ⇒ more carbonic acid ⇒ more acidic oceans ⇒ seashells dissolve

Modeling studies show that the pH of the oceans would need to drop by two full units, or to a pH of 6.0, for carbonate to dissolve at current temperatures (Segalstad 2008). Even the most extreme projections of decreasing alkalinity do not forecast that the oceans will approach neutral, let alone become truly acidic.

These models can predict pH in the controlled settings of a university laboratory, but not so much in the real world. The models do not take into account various processes which act to modify or "buffer" any increase in carbonic acid. The primary buffering agents are the chemical reactions of limestones and other minerals in ocean water. Limestones ($CaCO_3$) are among the primary rocks exposed on the surface of the Earth and beneath her oceans. Their presence guarantees that under modern conditions the oceans cannot become acidic—and certainly nowhere near as acidic as the rainwater that falls on them daily.

Carbonic acid reacts to limestones on land and at sea to increase the alkalinity, and add calcium to streams and oceans. Other minerals also add significant buffering as a backstop to the limestone reactions. According to Idso (2014), "they constitute an almost infinite buffer capacity."

Several other important factors act to buffer changes in ocean pH, but are not included in the models. For instance, warmer water and increasing CO_2 are expected to increase algal photosynthesis, which has been shown to *increase the alkalinity* of the ocean significantly. Some climate modelers are all too anxious to include variables which fit their preconceived notions, calling them "multiplier effects," but conveniently avoid them when they might disprove their theories. Note that, even with the most radical modeling of lower pH, the oceans remain significantly alkaline and cannot even approach neutrality at pH 7.0.

The terminology used is critically important. Climate extremists do not talk of a *"slight decrease in alkalinity."* That would not strike fear into the gullible hearts of the environmental fringe, for whom environmentalism appears to have become a substitute for true religion. Another way that the lessening of pH could be described would be to say that the oceans are becoming "less caustic." That, however, would put a positive spin on the matter, not at all what the alarmists intend. The term "ocean acidification" conveys the notion of a looming oceanic catastrophe, and it is on this basis that alarmists promote substantial and needless increases in the cost and regulation of energy.

Before we look at the science which will categorically disprove the notion of ocean "acidification," we should first look at some of the studies that peddle the doomsday scenario.

The most widely referenced chart concerning "acidification" is a comparison of the pH and dissolved CO_2 in the area north of Hawaii (Figure II-42). It shows a slight decline in pH and a steady increase of CO_2 over a period of nearly 30 years. As we shall see in Figure II-44, pH has been rising and falling in 50-year cycles with the last peak of alkalinity occurring in the mid-1960s, This 30-year record is just not long enough to make confident predictions about long-term trends.

A controversial and widely cited paper on the subject is Feely (2006), showing a graph linking decreasing pH to increasing CO_2. The graph shows "historic" and projected pH from 1850 to 2100, and the chart predicts that by 2100 pH levels will be down to 7.9 (which, incidentally, would still be quite alkaline). Unfortunately, while the graph is still available on the NOAA website (Feeley 2006) neither NOAA nor the author would provide permissions to use in this book.

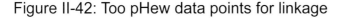

Figure II-42: Too pHew data points for linkage

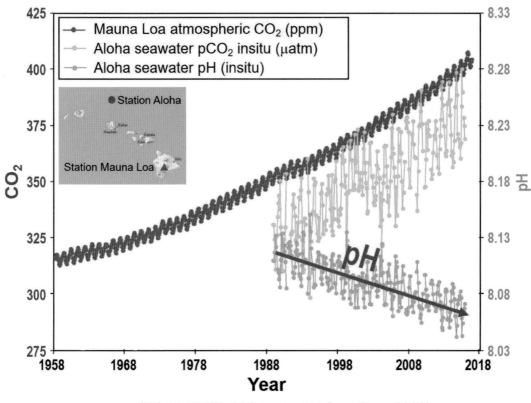

(NOAA PMEL 2017, adapted from Dore 2009)

Here is why:

In 2010 this work earned the author a trip to testify to Congress and a Heinz Family Foundation award worth $100,000. The citation said: "Ocean acidity is now considered global warming's 'evil twin,' thanks in large measure to Dr. Feely's seminal research on the changing ocean chemistry and its impact on marine ecosystems."

An enterprising, young PhD candidate at the University of New Mexico by the name of Mike Wallace looked closely into the work of Feely and his co-authors, finding that the supposedly "historic" data was nothing of the sort. Wallace observed that Feeley had only used real-world, measured data from 1990 to 2015. He had ignored real-world measurements dating back at least a century.

Feeley's graph was generated using climate modeling for the pre-1990 portion of the curve, rather than the actual measurements. When Wallace graphed the actual data, the "acidifying" trend produced by the model disappeared.

Wallace questioned Feely's co-author, Sabine, about why real-world measurements had been ignored. He was told that, if he continued his line of questioning, "You will not last long in your career." Wallace had this to say about these studies that provide the very basis of the ocean acidification argument: "In whose professional world is it acceptable to omit the majority of the data and also not to disclose the omission to any other soul or Congressional body? (Noon 2016)"

In a true scientific inquiry, *real data should always trump models.* If actual hard data are available, there is no need to forecast—unless your objective is to promote the latest hobgoblin of climate alarmism.

The Historical Record

Just as we saw when reviewing data on temperature and carbon dioxide, the historical record of what has happened in the real world is a signpost to the future. The long-term geologic history reveals some very inconvenient facts for climate alarmists spreading fear that acidic oceans will dissolve sea-shells. Data from the early climate certainly provide no basis for any such fear.

Liu (2009) examined corals in the South China Sea and reconstructed the pH history for the last 7,000 years. Figure II-43 shows the data from that study and compares it to the CO_2 history of the same period taken from the Vostok ice core, Antarctica. First, it is apparent that the current pH values and the rate of decrease are neither unprecedented nor unusual. In fact, the lowest measured alkalinity was about 6,000 years ago, when CO_2 levels were one-third below today's levels. The behavior of the real-world ocean is just the opposite of the behavior predicted by the IPCC and the merchants of climate doom.

Inconvenient Fact 55

There is no historic correlation between CO_2 and oceanic pH

Pelejero studied the pH history of a reef in the southwestern Pacific Ocean that provided nearly 300 years of pH data (2005). He found large changes in pH that varied over 50-year cycles (Figure II-44). We are nearing the end of a 50-year downtrend in pH and, if the cycles continue, we may see an increase in alkalinity, rather than the "acidification" predicted by alarmists. The authors noted that there was "no notable trend" toward lower boron values (boron is a proxy for pH). Also note that the most recent peak in alkalinity, from 1955 to 1970, occurred despite the fact that CO_2 emissions had already begun to increase significantly.

Figure II-43: 7,000 years of ocean pH in the South China Sea, and CO_2

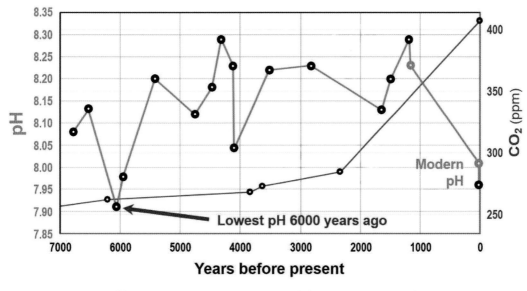

(Source data: pH: Liu 2009; CO_2: Barnola 2003)

Figure II-44: Reconstructed pH history of SW Pacific reef, 1708 – 1988

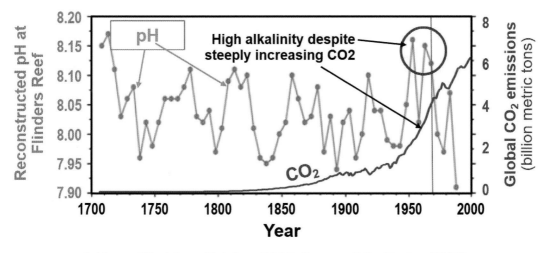

(pH: modified from Pelejero 2005; Source CO_2: Boden 2016)

Limestone, one of the most abundant sedimentary rocks on Earth, is calcium carbonate, as are the shells and exoskeletons of the creatures allegedly threatened by ocean "acidification." Limestone is precipitated from warm ocean waters that are supersaturated with calcium. Break open a piece of limestone and you are likely to find many fossils of the forerunners of modern creatures, these ancient creatures also needed alkaline water to prosper. Therefore, we can use the record of limestone deposits to see if acidification took place during periods of high CO_2 concentration.

During the Cambrian, Ordovician and Silurian periods of the early Paleozoic era (541 – 416 million years ago), CO_2 usually exceeded 4,000 ppm, reaching a maximum of nearly 8,000 ppm in the Cambrian Period. The latter was ~20 times today's concentration. When we compare CO_2 levels to the rock record from the author's home turf in the Appalachian Basin of the eastern United States (Fig. II-45), we find that most of these CO_2-enriched periods were dominated by limestone deposition (Fig II-46). Limestone deposition could not have occurred had the oceans been "acidified." Most of the limestone was deposited during the periods of highest CO_2 concentration.

Inconvenient Fact 56

The oceans did not become acidic even with CO_2 at 15 times modern levels.

Professor Ove Hoegh-Guldberg, Director of the Global Change Institute and Professor of Marine Science at the University of Queensland, and an advocate of politically driven science, had this to say concerning ocean "acidification":

> *When CO_2 levels in the atmosphere reach about 500 parts per million, you put calcification out of business in the oceans.*

The fossil record unambiguously shows that this statement is false. Perhaps the good professor should have walked down the hall and discussed his musings with one of the many distinguished geology professors at the university before uttering a statement so easily and decisively disproved by the rock record.

Proponents of ocean acidification focus only on the imagined harmful effects on sea-shells and corals from a supposed significant reduction in ocean pH—a decrease that we have seen is not at all likely. They ignore the many reputable studies that have identified the benefits of increasing CO_2 on oceanic plants, algae and animals, all of which would not be here today unless they had already long possessed the ability to adapt to far greater changes in pH than we are capable of causing.

The rational observer would ask:

> Why were the oceans not acidified during geological periods when the Earth's atmosphere carried up to 20 times today's CO_2 concentration?

> Did the processes which led to the proposed "acidification" really only begin with the Industrial Revolution?

Figure II-45: Limestone was deposited when the CO_2 concentration was extremely high.

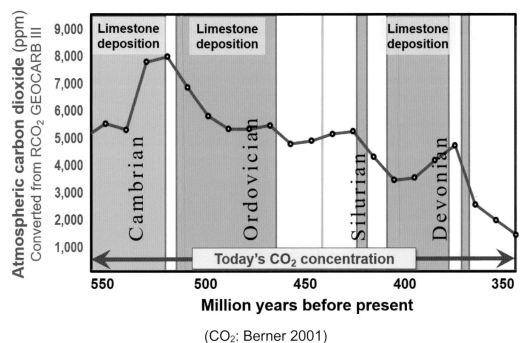

(CO$_2$: Berner 2001)

Figure II-46: Ordovician Black River carbonates laid down when CO_2 was 12 times today's concentration

(PA DCNR 2017)

Summary — Ocean Acidity

Predictions of the end of the oceans as we know them from "acidification" are based entirely on models that assume that oceans possess no organisms, rocks or dissolved solids that might moderate or buffer any increase in carbonic acid. Based on the fossil record and paleo-reconstructions of pH levels, we know that acidification of the oceans did not occur in the past even during times with CO_2 levels many multiples of today.

Unless entirely new oceanic chemical processes not yet evident in the burgeoning scientific literature on ocean "acidification" have mysteriously begun to operate at the beginning of the Industrial Revolution, the oceans will not become "acidified." The prognosticators of climate apocalypse are wrong again.

Sea-Level Rise — King Canute Couldn't Stop It — Nor Can We

Entire nations could be wiped off the face of the Earth by rising sea levels if the global warming trend is not reversed by the year 2000. Coastal flooding and crop failures would create an exodus of 'eco-refugees,' threatening political chaos.

— Noel Brown, UN official, June 30, 1989

Sea-level rise may be the most feared calamity associated with global warming. Because areas that would be affected have large and growing populations and include many of the world's economic centers, significant increases in the sea level could be devastating. Media reports of flooded cities and coastlines after storms are all too often linked to global warming and rising sea levels. Nearly every group spreading climate fear prominently features the specter of flooding from rising oceans.

Media sensationalism is compounded by misrepresentations of available science and by an unscientific reliance on computer projections rather than on historical data.

A report for the United Nations' Environment Program in 2005 asserted that there would be 50 million climate refugees by 2010, many of them driven out of their coastal homes by sea-level rise (Myers 2005). The UN even provided a handy identifier map which included the areas of highest risk: low-lying islands of the Pacific and Caribbean, and commented that "some will disappear completely." Since their predictions have proven so completely incorrect, the map has since been removed from their website in order not to thoroughly discredit any of their subsequent, similarly outrageous, predictions.

In 2011, Gavin Atkins of the *Asian Correspondent* asked, "What happened to the climate refugees?" and provided updated population numbers for some of the most at-risk island nations which the UN had predicted would be under water now:

Bahamas: the 2010 census showed an increase in population of >50,000 persons in 10 years;

St. Lucia: 5 per cent increase in population 2001 to 2010;

Seychelles: the number of persons grew by >6,500 from 2002 to 2010;

Solomon Islands: there were 100,000 more people from 2001 to 2010.

So rather than citizens fleeing these "at-risk" islands, they appear to be thriving quite nicely on islands which are a refuge for those persons leaving the cold of northern climes.

Undeterred by facts or common sense, the UN is now predicting the same 50 million climate refugees by the updated timeline of 2020. We won't have to wait long now to see how that prediction turns out.

Sea Level — Science, Facts and Data

Over the last six million years of severe icehouse conditions, the primary driver of sea-level changes were periodic episodes of glaciation. These locked up huge amounts of water—mainly in the northern latitudes—drawing down sea levels. During warmer interglacial stages, melting ice yielded markedly higher seas. According to the U.S. Geological Survey, the peak glaciation of the last ice age about 20,000 years ago produced sea levels about 400 feet (140 m) lower than today. Since that point, the climate has warmed and glaciers have melted, returning water from the land to the oceans.

Figure II-47 shows reconstructed sea levels dating back to the latter part of our most recent ice age (Waelbroeck 2002). This chart is plotted with data on 1,500-year intervals, so it does not capture the detail that later figures provide. It does show that the most rapid rise occurred during the first 6,000 to 8,000 years of warming, as the climate transitioned from the ice age to the interglacial period. Then the rate of rise slowed to a relative stability that has endured, more or less, to the present.

Figure II-47: 20,000-year sea level reconstruction

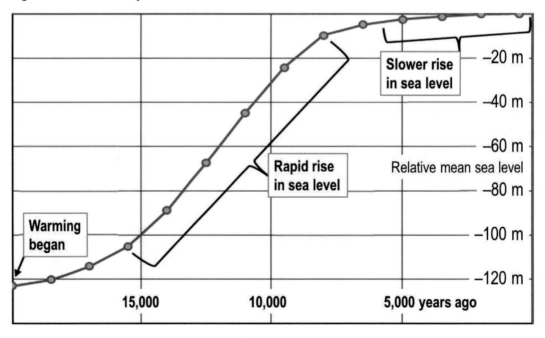

(Source data: Waelbroeck 2002)

Inconvenient Fact 57

Sea-level increase began >15,000 years ago.

The sea level actually *fell* during the cold of the Little Ice Age, but then resumed its long-term rise in the late 1700s, in response to the warming coming out of the depths of the Little Ice Age (Figure II-48). Acceleration of sea-level rise kicked in during the mid-1850s and has remained nearly constant since that time. Bear in mind that the re-initiation and acceleration of the rise began at times when human-created CO_2 could not have had any significant effect on temperatures.

Between 1901 and 2010, the rise amounted to about 7.5 inches (190 mm) or 0.07 inches (1.8 mm) per year (Houston 2011). The seas began to rise long before we began our post-World War II increase in CO_2 emissions. This natural sea-level rise will continue whether or not we reduce our greenhouse-gas emissions.

Since the sea level has been rising for more than 15,000 years, the question to ask is not, "Is it rising?" but, "Is it rising *faster?*" Most climate models predict faster sea-level rise, but tide gauges, which are the most reliable long-term measurement of rise show no detectable acceleration since we began adding appreciable amounts of CO_2 to the air in the mid-20th Century.

Satellite altimetry—measuring the sea level by satellites—was introduced in 1993 and sea-level rise measured from them shows an acceleration of rise. There is evidence, however, that the raw satellite data was adjusted so as to produce the desired acceleration (Mörner, 2011); and the inter-calibration errors between the successive generations of satellites exceed the total sea-level rise the satellites purport to measure. The bottom line? The combination of short time frame, calibration errors and apparent manipulation of the satellite data provide too many questions for us to use this information with any confidence.

Inconvenient Fact 58

Recent sea-level rise began 150 years before the increase in CO_2.

Contrary to the predictions of the IPCC and other noted experts, numerous studies have reported that the sea level is not rising faster. Many others have documented a slower rise (Holgate 2007; Mörner 2011; Houston 2011). What is undeniable is that IPCC has been compelled to reduce its sea-level predictions in each successive five-year *Assessment Report* (Fig. II-49).

Figure II-48: More than 200 Years of sea-level rise

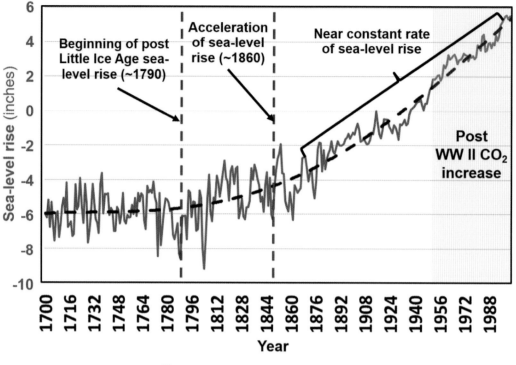

(Source data: Jevrejeva 2008)

Figure II-49: Sea-level rise predictions are failing.

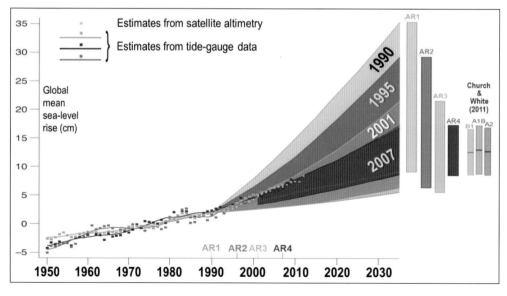

(Modified from IPCC 2013, fig. 1.10)

Holgate (2007) reviewed nine long-term records (1904 – 2003) worldwide, and found that the rate of sea-level rise *decreased* from 1950 onward (Fig. II-50).

Figure II-50: Global average sea level from nine records shows decreasing rate of sea-level rise.

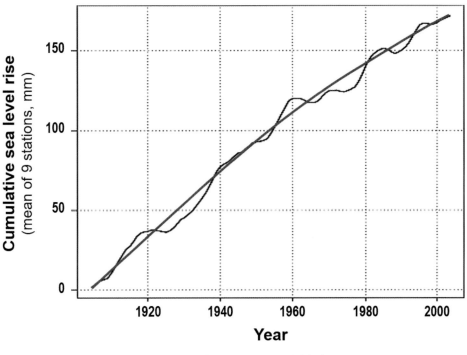

(Adapted from Holgate 2007)

A landmark study of Australian sea-level rise in 2011 (Figure II-51) reported that the data "reveals (sic) a consistent trend of weak *deceleration* at each of these gauge sites throughout Australasia over the period from 1940 to 2000." So, contrary to frightening predictions of a rising rate of increase, we find just the opposite may be occurring.

Further confirmation of a possible deceleration of sea-level rise was a study of 83 tide gauges by Houston and Dean (2011). Their conclusions were extremely incon-venient for those predicting the inundation of Miami:

Our analyses do not indicate acceleration in sea level in U.S. tide gauge records during the 20th century. Instead, for each time period we consider, the records show small decelerations that are consistent with a number of earlier studies of worldwide-gauge records.

Figure II-51: Sea-level rise at Australian tide gauges is slowing.

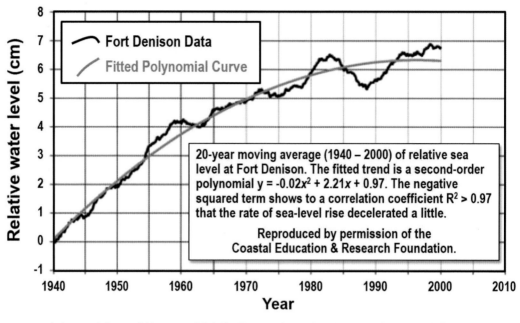

Adapted from (Watson 2011). Reproduced with permission of CERF

One of the most common climate myths is that the melting of the northern polar ice cap will not only lead to the extinction of polar bears, but cause significant sea-level rise. Actually, the entire north polar ice cap could melt and the change in the global sea level would be virtually zero. That is because the ice cap is frozen seawater, floating in the Arctic Ocean. As the ice melts, water displaces the void left by the formerly frozen H_2O, most of which is submerged. According to the U.S. Coast Guard, seven-eighths of an iceberg is beneath the ocean surface. (Think of the Titanic, and see Figure II-52).

Inconvenient Fact 59

Melting the northern polar ice cap would not increase the sea level.

Sea-level change is driven mainly by the melting or accumulation of ice in land-based mountain or continental glaciers. The bulk of the water created by the melting of this type of glacier or ice sheet will eventually find its way to the oceans and cause the level of the sea to rise to some degree. During ice ages, large amounts of water were locked up in the glaciers covering primarily the northern latitudes of North America, Europe and Asia, lowering the level significantly.

Figure II-52: A sea-level test

The important fact that if floating ice melts it does not raise the level of the sea can be tested by putting some ice cubes in a glass and filling it to a marked level with water.

Even after the ice melts, the water level is unchanged.

Antarctica today has nine-tenths of the world's land-based ice mass. (Greenland has much of the rest.) Paradoxically, Antarctica is also the Earth's driest continent. Water vapor across the continent is often near zero, and very little snow actually falls. The little that does precipitate stays there, and for a very long time, having built up over hundreds of thousands of years to a thickness of more than ten thousand feet in some areas.

So the world's driest continent has the greatest potential to drive sea-level rise.

Well-publicized reports of melting ice shelves surrounding the Antarctic Peninsula have been driving an untrue narrative of a melting Antarctica. The ice shelves are, like the northern ice cap, afloat. Complete melting of these would have no effect on the sea level. The media-driven hype on this subject climaxed after a portion of the Larsen C Ice Shelf broke away in Mid-July, 2017 and Antarctica became the poster child of alarm about warmer weather.

> *The Larsen C crack is only a symptom of a larger problem. Taken together, recent findings show troubling changes are happening almost everywhere across Antarctica's massive icy expanse.*
> — Brian Kahn, Climate Central, May 2017

> *With 10 per cent of the world's population, or 700 million people, living less than 10 metres above present sea level, an additional three metres of sea level rise from the Antarctic alone will have a profound impact on us all.*
> — Dr. Nick Golledge, senior research fellow,
> Antarctic Research Centre, Victoria.

Why the focus specifically on the Antarctic Peninsula? Alarmists do this because it appears to be the only area of the continent that is warming. Numerous studies have reported cooling across the bulk of the Antarctic continent, with the lone outlier being the Antarctic Peninsula (Comiso 2000, Doran 2002). The Peninsula, however, represents only about 2% of the Antarctic land mass (Figure II-53).

Figure II-53: The Antarctic

This Landsat image mosaic of Antarctica (by permission of NASA, 2017) shows the Antarctic Peninsula at upper left. The peninsula represents little more than 2% of the land mass of the world's driest continent.

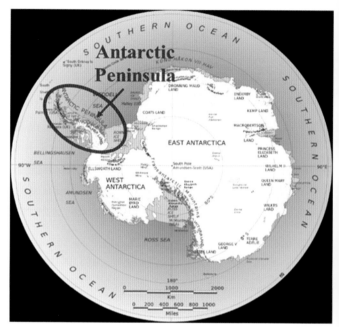

Inconvenient Fact 60

Most of Antarctica is cooling and gaining ice mass.

The cooling of the majority of the continent has increased, rather than decreased, the area of sea ice surrounding the Antarctic continent (Fig. II-54). The cooling and consequent ice growth is not what the climate modelers had predicted.

IPCC's latest high-end projection (IPCC 2013), while much lower than their previous prognostications, is that the sea level may rise at almost half an inch per year, or more than 3 feet (11 m) by 2100. This is nearly 6 times our currently very steady rate of 0.07 inches/year (1.8 mm). Once again, those advancing a vision of climate apocalypse rely on questionable models, instead of looking at the data to see what is actually happening.

Figure II-54: Increasing Antarctic sea-ice area

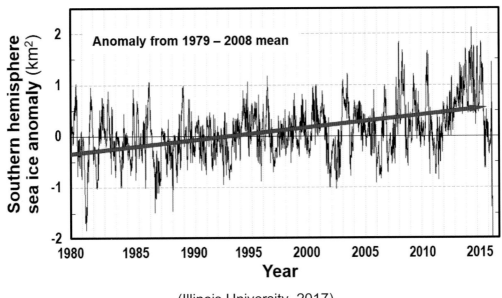

(Illinois University, 2017)

Sea-level rise, which began long before widespread use of fossil fuels, will continue until the next ice age. And may God help us when that day arrives. Cold is a killer, where heat, on the whole, is not.

Legislation enacted to halt the rise of the seas would be no more effective today than it was almost a millennium ago, when King Canute demonstrated the limits of government power to his courtiers by having his throne set up by the seashore and commanding the sea not to rise. The tide came in as usual.

In 2008, upon receiving the nomination for president, Barack Obama stated that we could tell future generations, "This was the moment when the rise of the oceans began to slow."

King Canute at the shore

Well, he may have been correct, but certainly not because, Canute-like, he had stretched forth his trembling hand over the ocean and commanded the sea not to rise.

Summary — The Benefits of Principled Inaction

The inconvenient facts in this book support quite a different narrative from that offered by proponents of apocalyptic human-driven climate change. On every key topic examined, the evidence, supported by voluminous peer reviewed studies, reveals that the "consensus" opinion promoted by climate-apocalypse proponents is consistently at odds with reality. In chapter after chapter, we learned that scientifically supported truths, as revealed within *"Inconvenient Facts,"* are polar opposites of what we hear from climate alarmists and their willing accomplices in the media.

Rather than a world quickly diving into a man-made climate hell from which we cannot return, the Earth, its ecosystems, and we humans are, instead, thriving. We are thriving *because* of increasing CO_2 and rising temperatures *not in spite* of it.

By every metric reviewed, we have seen that the current changing climate has led to increasing food production, soil moisture, crop growth and a "greening" of the Earth. All the while droughts, forest fires, heat waves and temperature-related deaths have declined substantially. Only the radical worldview of the environmental extremist could ignore benefits clearly being accrued from atmospheric changes while embracing harmful economic policies based on failed climate models.

Yes, there is such a thing as the greenhouse effect. Yes, there has been some warming. Yes, some of the warming is likely man-made. Yes, some further man-made warming is to be expected. On all these matters, few would disagree, for they are all demonstrable.

But no, past and future anthropogenic warming does not mean that catastrophe will follow, or that measures to prevent global warming are scientifically and economically justified, or that capitalism should be blamed for the supposed "crisis"— still less that it should be destroyed because of spurious science.

From the Inconvenient Facts we have reviewed, *the first and most important conclusion is that the correct policy to address the non-problem of man-made global warming is to have the courage to do nothing.* In this case, it takes courage to do nothing. Imagine the enormous pressure on President Trump to keep the United States in the Paris climate accord. Worldwide indignation and scorn were heaped on him after his decision to withdraw from the agreement, yet it was the correct and courageous one to make. For leaders supporting the Paris agreement, the specter of catastrophic warming provides the moral justification for ever-higher taxation, ever-tighter regulation, ever-greater state interference and ever-diminished private freedom.

Thanks to near-total control of the news media by proponents of a pending Thermageddon, critical truths are poorly understood and even derided: the truth that there is no "consensus", the truth that "consensus" would not matter even if it existed, the truth that global warming will be small and largely beneficial, the truth that preventing it would be orders of magnitude costlier than adapting to it, the truth that the correct policy is to have the courage to do nothing.

Yet, like it or not, the truth is the truth. Policy should, in the end, be based on objective truth and not on the back of a lavishly-funded and elaborate international campaign of crafty—and profitable for some—falsehoods promoted by the political, financial, corporate, bureaucratic and media establishments.

Too many scientists have failed to uphold the integrity of their profession, whether because of willful self-promotion, desperate self-preservation, ignorance, greed, or fear of ridicule by the high priests of climate orthodoxy. They have shirked their duty to resist the campaign of lies and libels perpetrated by a small but influential number of their colleagues. It will take science many decades to overcome the damage wrought by this corruption of the scientific community.

If this book can help alert the establishment to the Inconvenient Facts that Al Gore and his ilk have found it expedient and profitable to ignore or to deny, then perhaps steps can be taken towards the urgent restoration of the primacy of truth in science—and in society.

List of Inconvenient Facts

Inconvenient Fact 1
Carbon dioxide is not the primary greenhouse gas.

Inconvenient Fact 2
The warming effect of CO_2 declines as its concentration increases.

Inconvenient Fact 3
First and foremost, CO_2 is plant food.

Inconvenient Fact 4
In last four ice ages, the CO_2 level was dangerously low.

Inconvenient Fact 5
140-million-year trend of dangerously decreasing CO_2

Inconvenient Fact 6
Our current geologic period (Quaternary) has the lowest average CO_2 levels in the history of the Earth.

Inconvenient Fact 7
More CO_2 means more plant growth.

Inconvenient Fact 8
More CO_2 helps to feed more people worldwide.

Inconvenient Fact 9
More CO_2 means moister soil.

Inconvenient Fact 10
Recent Inconvenient Pause of 18 years in warming, despite rise in CO_2

Inconvenient Fact 11
CO_2 rose after the Second World War, but temperature fell.

REALLY Inconvenient Fact 12
Modern warming began long before SUVs or coal-fired plants.

Inconvenient Fact 13
Melting glaciers and rising seas confirm warming predated increases of CO_2.

Inconvenient Fact 14
Temperatures have changed for 800,000 years. It wasn't us.

Inconvenient Fact 15
Interglacials usually last 10,000-15,000 years. Ours is 11,000 years old.

Inconvenient Fact 16
Each of the four previous inter-glacial warming periods were significantly warmer than our current temperature.

Inconvenient Fact 17
The last interglacial, ~120,000 years ago, was 8ºC (14.4ºF) warmer than today. The polar bears survived. Greenland didn't melt.

Inconvenient Fact 18
Temperatures changed during the past 10,000 years. It wasn't us.

Inconvenient Fact 19
Today's total warming and warming rate are similar to earlier periods.

Inconvenient Fact 20
It was warmer than today for 6,100 of the last 10,000 years.

Inconvenient Fact 21
Our current trend is neither unusual nor unprecedented.

Inconvenient Fact 22
Earth's orbit and tilt drive glacial-interglacial changes.

Inconvenient Fact 23
We are living in one of the coldest periods in all of Earth's history.

Inconvenient Fact 24
Earth has not had a geologic period this cold in 250 million years.

Inconvenient Fact 25
The only thing constant about temperatures over 600 million years is that they have been constantly changing.
(this is a recurring Inconvenient Fact)

Inconvenient Fact 26
For most of Earth's history, it was about 10 °C (18 °F) warmer than today.

Inconvenient Fact 27
IPCC models overstate future warming up to three times too much.

Inconvenient Fact 28
For human advancement, warmer is better than colder.

Inconvenient Fact 29
A return to the temperature at the beginning of the Industrial Revolution would lead to famine and death.

Inconvenient Fact 30
Only 0.3% of published scientists stated in their papers that recent warming was mostly man-made.

Inconvenient Fact 31
Science is not consensus and consensus is not science.

Inconvenient Fact 32
More CO_2 ⇒ fewer droughts

Inconvenient Fact 33
Higher temperature ⇒ fewer droughts

Inconvenient Fact 34
Forest fires across the northern hemisphere are decreasing.

Inconvenient Fact 35
More CO_2 » CO_2 fertilization » more soil moisture » faster tree growth » fewer forest fires

Inconvenient Fact 36
More CO_2 in the atmosphere means more food for everyone.

Inconvenient fact 37
The Earth is becoming greener, not turning into desert.

Inconvenient Fact 38
Growing seasons are lengthening.

Inconvenient Fact 39
More CO_2 and warmer weather mean more world food production.

Inconvenient Fact 40
EPA: Heat waves are not becoming more frequent.

Inconvenient Fact 41
Extreme heat events are declining.

Inconvenient Fact 42
Cold kills far more people every year than heat.

Inconvenient Fact 43
Warmer weather means many fewer temperature-related deaths.

Inconvenient Fact 44
Warmer weather prevents millions of premature deaths each year.

Inconvenient Fact 45
More CO_2 and warmth mean shorter, less intense heat waves.

Inconvenient Fact 46
Number of tornadoes is declining.

Inconvenient Fact 47
The number of tornadoes in 2016 was the lowest on record.

Inconvenient Fact 48
Deaths from tornadoes are falling.

Inconvenient Fact 49
There has been no increase in frequency of hurricanes in recent data.

Inconvenient Fact 50
We have seen 250 years of declining hurricane frequency.

Inconvenient Fact 51
No significant increase in hurricane intensity due to warming

Inconvenient Fact 52
The population of polar bears is growing.

Inconvenient Fact 53
There are more polar bears than we've had for 50 years.

Inconvenient Fact 54
Polar bears are thriving even where sea ice is diminishing.

Inconvenient Fact 55
There is no historic correlation between CO_2 and oceanic pH.

Inconvenient Fact 56
The oceans did not become acidic even at 15 times modern CO_2 levels.

Inconvenient Fact 57
Sea-level increase began >15,000 years ago.

Inconvenient Fact 58
Recent sea-level rise began 150 years before the increase in CO_2.

Inconvenient Fact 59
Melting the northern polar ice cap would not increase sea level.

Inconvenient Fact 60
Most of Antarctica is cooling and gaining ice mass.

References

Alley RB (2004) GISP2 Ice Core Temperature and Accumulation Data. IGBP PAGES/World Data Center for Paleoclimatology Data Contribution Series #2004-013. NOAA/NGDC Paleoclimatology Program, Boulder CO, USA. ftp://ftp.ncdc.noaa.gov/pub/data/paleo/icecore/greenland/summit/gisp2/isotopes/gisp2_temp_accum_alley2000.txt

Atkins G (2011) What happened to the climate refugees? Asian Correspondent, https://asiancorrespondent.com/2011/04/what-happened-to-the-climate-refugees/#BaTVoqe4ZRMjLr7K.97

Barnola JM, Raynaud D, Lorius C et al (2003) Historical CO_2 record from the Vostok ice core. In Trends: A Compendium of Data on Global Change. CDIAC, Oak Ridge National Laboratory, U.S. Dept of Energy, Oak Ridge, TN, USA, http://cdiac.ornl.gov/ftp/trends/co2/vostok.icecore.co2

Bastasch M (2017) So-called '97%' global warming 'consensus' number is a hoax: real number is 32.6%. Daily Caller News Foundation http://dailycaller.com/2017/03/05/lets-talk-about-the-97-consensus-on-global-warming

Behringer W (2007) A Cultural History of Climate. Polity Press translation 2010, Malden MA

Berner RA, Kothavala Z (2001) GEOCARB III: A revised model of atmospheric CO_2 over Phanerozoic time, IGBP PAGES and World Data Center for Paleoclimatology, Data Contribution Series # 2002-051. NOAA/NGDC Paleoclimatology Program, Boulder CO, USA.

Blake ES, Landsea CW, Gibney EJ (2011) The deadliest, costliest, and most intense united states tropical cyclones from 1851 to 2010 (and other frequently requested hurricane facts) NOAA National Weather Service, National Hurricane Center, Miami, Florida

Boden TA, Marland G, Andres RJ (2013) Global, regional and national fossil-fuel CO_2 emissions. CDIAC, Oak Ridge National Laboratory, U.S. Dept of Energy, Oak Ridge, TN, USA, doi:10.3334/CDIAC/00001_V2013

Boden TA, Marland G, Andres RJ (2016) Global CO_2 emissions from Fossil-Fuel Burning Cement Manufacture and Gas Flaring 1751 - 2013. CDIAC, Oak Ridge National Laboratory, U.S. Dept of Energy, Oak Ridge, TN, USA, DOI 10.3334/CDIAC/00001_V2010

Boden T, Andres B (2017) Ranking of the world's countries by 2014 total CO2 emissions from fossil-fuel burning, cement production, and gas flaring. Emissions (CO2_TOT) are expressed in thousand metric tons of carbon (not CO2), Carbon Dioxide Information Analysis Center, Oak Ridge National Laboratory

Bornay E (2007) Atlas environnement 2007 du Monde diplomatique, Paris

Box JE, Yang L, Bromwich DH, Bai L (2009) Greenland Ice Sheet Surface Air Temperature Variability: 1840 – 2007*. American Meteorological Society, Journal of Climate Vol 22, pp 4029–4049

Browman HI (2016) Applying organized scepticism to ocean acidification research, ICES Journal of Marine Science 73 (3): 529–536

Brown T (2011) The long, slow thaw. Climate etc. website https://judith-curry.com/2011/12/01/the-long-slow-thaw/

Calder N (1975) In the Grip of a New Ice Age. International Wildlife, July 1975

Carter R (2011) Climate: The Counter Consensus, Stacey International, London England

CDIAC (2016) Recent Greenhouse Gas Concentrations. Carbon Dioxide Information Analysis Center http://cdiac.ornl.gov/pns/current_ghg.html

Christy J (2015) That stubborn climate. University of Alabama at Huntsville, http://training.ua.edu/almineral/_documents/JohnChristy.pdf

Christy J, U.S. House Committee on Science, Space & Technology 2 Feb 2016, Testimony of John R. Christy University of Alabama in Huntsville.

Ciscar, J, Watkiss P, Hunt A, Pye S, Horrocks L (2009) Climate change impacts in Europe, Final report of the PESETA research project, JRC Scientific and Technical Reports, European Commission Joint Research Centre Institute for Prospective Technological Studies

Comiso JC (2000) Variability and trends in Antarctic surface temperatures from in situ and satellite infrared measurements. J Clim 13:1674–1696

Cook ER, Seager R, Cane MA (2007) North American drought: reconstructions, causes, and consequences. Earth-Sci Rev 81(1):93–134, doi:10.1016/j.earscirev.2006.12.002

Cook J, Nuccitelli D, Green SA et al (2013) Quantifying the consensus on anthropogenic global warming in the scientific literature. Environ Res Lett 8(2):024024

Crockford SJ (2015) Polar bear population estimates, 1960 – 2017. wp.me/p2CaNn-gP2

Dahl-Jensen D, et al, (2013) Eemian interglacial reconstructed from a Greenland folded ice core. Nature, 493, p 489–494 doi:10.1038/nature11789

de Jong R, de Bruin S, de Wit A et al (2011) Analysis of monotonic greening and browning trends from global normalized-difference vegetation index time series, Remote Sens Env 115:692–702, doi:10.1016/j.rse.2010.10.011

de Jong R, Schaepman ME, Furrer R et al (2013) Spatial relationship between climatologies and changes in global vegetation activity. Glob Change Biol 19:1953 – 1964, doi:10.1111/gcb.12193

De Saussure N (1804) Chemical research on plant matter

Davis RE, Knappenberger PC, Michaels PJ, Novicoff WM (2003) Changing heat-related mortality in the United States. Environmental Health Perspectives, 111, 1712-1718.

Dore JE, Lukas R, Sadler DW, Church MJ, Karl DM (2009) Physical and biogeochemical modulation of ocean acidification in the central North Pacific. Proceeding of the National Academy of Sciences, Vol 106, No 30   doi: 10.1073/pnas.0906044106

Doran PT, Priscu JC, Lyons WB et al (2002) Antarctic climate cooling and terrestrial ecosystem response. Nature, doi: 10.1038/nature710

Doswell CA, Moller AR, Brooks HE (1999) Storm spotting and public awareness since the first tornado forecasts of 1948. Weather & Forecasting 14(4): 544–557

Driessen P (2014) Miracle molecule — carbon dioxide, gas of life. Committee for a Constructive Tomorrow, Washington DC

Durner GM, Douglas DC, Albeke SE, Whiteman JP, Amstrup SC, Richardson E, Wilson RR, Ben-David M (2017) Increased Arctic sea ice drift alters adult female polar bear movements and energetics. Glob Change Biol. 2017; 00:1–14. https://doi.org/10.1111/gcb.13746

Earle S (2017) Physical Geology by Steven Earle used under a CC-BY 4.0 international license. Chapter 16.1 Glacial Periods in Earth's History. In Geology/BC Open Textbook Project, https://opentextbc.ca/geology/chapter/16-1-glacial-periods-in-earths-history.

EPA (2016a) Palmer United States drought-severity index data. https://www.epa.gov/climate-indicators/climate-change-indicators-drought, accessed 2017 May 2

EPA (2016b) U.S. Annual Heat Wave Index 1895 – 2015, https://www.epa.gov/climate-indicators/climate-change-indicators-high-and-low-temperatures

Fagan B (2000) The Little Ice Age—How Climate Made History 1300 – 1850, Basic Books, NY, NY

Fall S, Watts A, Nielsen Gammon J, Jones E, Niyogi D, Christy JR, Pielke RA Sr (2011) Analysis of the impacts of station exposure on the US Historical Climatology Network temperatures and temperature trends, J. Geophys. Res., 116, D14120, doi:10.1029/2010JD015146

Feely RA, Doney SC, and Cooley SR (2009) Ocean acidification: Present conditions and future changes in a high-CO_2 world. Oceanography 22: 36–47.

Feely RA, Sabine CL, and Fabry VJ (2006) CARBON DIOXIDE AND OUR OCEAN LEGACY, NOAA Pacific Marine Environmental Laboratory http://www.pmel.noaa.gov/pubs/PDF/feel2899/feel2899.pdf

Fischer EM, Seneviratne SI, Lüthi D, et al (2007a) Contribution of land-atmosphere coupling to recent European summer heatwaves. Geophys Res Lett 34

Fischer EM, Seneviratne, Vidale PL et al (2007b) Soil moisture-atmosphere interactions during the 2003 European summer heatwave, J Clim 30(12)

Flannigan MD, Bereron Y, Engelmark O, Wotton BM (1998) Future wildfire in circum-boreal forest in relation to global warming, Journal of Vegetation Science 9, pp 469–476

Gasparrini A, Guo Y, Hashizume M, Lavigne E, Zanobetti A, Schwartz J, Tobias A, Tong S, Rocklöv J, Forsberg B, Leone M, De Sario M, Bell ML, Guo Y, Wu C, Kan H, Yi S, de Sousa M, Stagliorio Z, Hilario P, Saldiva N, Honda Y, Kim H, Armstrong B (2015) Mortality risk attributable to high and low ambient temperature: a multicountry observational study, The Lancet, Vol 386 July 25, 2015

Goklany IM (2009) Deaths and death rates from extreme weather events, 1900 – 2008. J Am Phys Surg 14(4):102–109

Gosselin AP (2013) Atmospheric CO_2 concentrations at 400 ppm are still dangerously low for life on Earth, http://notrickszone.com/2013/05/17/atmospheric-co2-concentrations-at-400-ppm-are-still-dangerously-low-for-life-on-earth/#sthash.qUYeTcPh.dpuf

Grinsted A, Moore JC, Jevrejeva S (2009), Reconstructing sea level from paleo and projected temperatures 200 to 2100AD. Clim. Dyn.

Grove JM (2001) The Initiation of the Little Ice Age in Regions around the North Atlantic. Climatic Change 48 pp 53–82

HadCRUT4 (2017) The Hadley Climate Research Unit (HadCRUT4) annual global mean surface temperature dataset, http://www.metoffice.gov.uk/hadobs/hadcrut4/data/current/download.html

Halevy I, Bachan A (2017) The geologic history of seawater pH. Science 355, 1069–1071 (2017) 10 March 2017

Hao Z, AghaKouchak A, Nakhjiri N et al (2014) Global integrated drought monitoring and prediction system. Sci Data 1, doi:10.1038/sdata.2014.1

Holgate SJ (2007) On the decadal rates of sea level change during the twentieth century. Geophys Res Lett 34:L01602, doi: 10.1029/2006GL028492

Holland G, and Webster P (2007) Heightened tropical cyclone activity in the North Atlantic: natural variability or climate trend? Phil Trans R Soc A doi:10.1098/rsta.2007.2083

Hoskins E (2014) The diminishing influence of increasing carbon dioxide on temperature. https://wattsupwiththat.com/2014/08/10/the-diminishing-influence-of-increasing-carbon-dioxide-on-temperature

Houghton JT, Ding Y, Griggs DJ, Noguer M, van der Linden PJ, Dai X, Maskell K, and IPCC (2007) Climate Change 2007: Contribution of Working Group I to the Fourth Assessment Report of the Intergovernmental Panel on Climate Change. IPCC, Geneva, Switzerland, p 115IPCC, 2001: Climate Change 2001: The Scientific Basis. Contribution of Working Group I to the Third Assessment Report of the Intergovernmental Panel on Climate Change

Houston JR, Dean RG (2011) Sea-level acceleration based on U.S. tide gauges and extensions of previous global gauge analyses. J Coast Res 27(3): 409–417

Idso CD (2013) The positive externalities of carbon dioxide. http://www.co2science.org/education/reports/co2benefits/MonetaryBenefitsofRisingCO2onGlobalFoodProduction.pdf

Idso CD, Idso SB, Carter RM et al [Eds] (2014) Climate change reconsidered II: biological impacts. Heartland Institute, Chicago, USA

Illinois, University of (2017) Cryosphere Today southern hemisphere sea-ice anomaly, 1979 – 2017. http://arctic.atmos.uiuc.edu/cryosphere/, accessed April 2017,

IPCC 1990 Climate Change The IPCC Scientific Assessment. Houghton, JT, Jenkins GJ, Ephraums JJ. Cambridge University Press, New York, Port Chester, Melbourne, Sydney, 365pp

IPCC (2001): Climate Change 2001: The Scientific Basis. Contribution of Working Group I to the Third Assessment Report of the Intergovernmental Panel on Climate Change [Houghton, J.T.,Y. Ding, D.J. Griggs, M. Noguer, P.J. van der Linden, X. Dai, K. Maskell, and C.A. Johnson (eds.)]. Cambridge University Press, Cambridge, United Kingdom and New York, NY, USA, 881pp.

IPCC (2007) Climate Change 2007: The Physical Science Basis. Contribution of Working Group I to the Fourth Assessment Report of the Intergovernmental Panel on Climate Change. Solomon S, Qin D, Manning M, Chen Z, Marquis M, Avery KB, Tignor M, Miller HL (eds.)]. Cambridge University Press, Cambridge, United Kingdom and New York, NY, USA, 996 pp.

IPCC (2013) Climate change 2013: The Physical Science Basis. Contribution of Working Group I to the Fifth Assessment Report of the Intergovernmental Panel on Climate Change [Stocker TF, Qin D, Plattner GK et al (eds)]. Cambridge University Press, Cambridge, United Kingdom & New York, NY, USA, 1535 pp.

Japan Meteorological Agency, Acidification in the Pacific, Otemachi, Chiyoda-ku, Tokyo 100–8122, Japan http://www.data.jma.go.jp/kaiyou/english/oa_pacific/oceanacidification_pacific_en.html

Jefferson T (1801) Notes on the State of Virginia. https://stevengoddard.wordpress.com/2011/02/22/1801-thomas-jefferson-notes-dramatic-climate-change-in-virginia/

Jevrejeva S, Moore JC, Grinsted A, Woodworth PL (2008) Recent global sea level acceleration started over 200 years ago? Geophys. Res. Lett., 35, L08715, doi:10.1029/2008GL033611

Jordan WC (1996) The Great Famine, Princeton, Princeton University Press, 20

Jouzel J, et al. (2007a) EPICA Dome C Ice Core 800K Yr Deuterium Data and Temperature Estimates. IGBP PAGES/World Data Center for Paleoclimatology Data Contribution Series # 2007-091. NOAA/NCDC Paleoclimatology Program, Boulder CO, USA.

Jouzel J et al. (2007b) Orbital and Millennial Antarctic Climate Variability over the Past 800,000 Years. Science, Vol. 317, No. 5839, pp.793–797, 10 August 2007.

Kalkstein LS, Greene S, Mills, DM, Samenow J (2011) An evaluation of the pro gress in reducing heat-related human mortality in major U.S. cities. Natural Hazards, 56, 113-129.

Kang N, & Elsner JB (2015) Trade-off between intensity and frequency of global tropical cyclones, Nature Climate Change, Letters

Keigwin LD (1996) The Little Ice Age and Medieval Warm Period in the Sargasso Sea *Science* 274, No. 5292, 1504–1508. ftp://ftp.ncdc.noaa.gov/pub/data/paleo/contributions_by_author/keigwin1996/

Kossin JP, Knapp KR, Vimont DJ, Harper BA (2007) Geophysical Research Letters volume 34 pages L04815 DOI : 10.1029/2006GL028836 http://nca2014.global-change.gov/search/node?search_api_views_fulltext=hurricane%20pdi

Landsea C (2007) Counting Atlantic tropical cyclones back to 1900, EOS Volume 88, Issue 18, pp 197–202

Landsea C (2011) Hurricanes and Global Warming. Opinion piece on NOAA website: http://www.aoml.noaa.gov/hrd/Landsea/gw_hurricanes/

Le Quéré C, Andres RJ, Boden T et al (2012) The global carbon budget 1959–2011. Earth System Science Data Discussions 5(2):1107–1157, doi: 10.5194/essdd-5-1107-2012

Legates DR, Soon W, Briggs WM (2013) Learning and Teaching Climate Science: The perils of consensus knowledge using agnotology. Sci Edu 22:2007–2017, doi:10.1007/s11191-013-9588-3

Legates DR, Soon W, Briggs WM et al (2015) Climate consensus and 'misinformation': a rejoinder to 'Agnotology, scientific consensus, and the teaching and learning of climate change. Sci Edu 24:299–318, doi: 10.1007/s11191-013-9647-9

Lisiecki LE, Raymo ME (2005) A Pliocene-Pleistocene stack of 57 globally distributed Benthic δ^{18} records. Paleoceanography, vol. 20, pa1003, doi:10.1029/2004PA001071

Liu Y, Liu W, Peng Z, Xiao Y, Wei G, Sun W, He J, Liu G, Chou C (2009) Instability of seawater pH in the South China Sea during the mid-late Holocene: Evidence from boron isotopic composition of corals, Geochimica et Cosmochimica Acta 73 (2009) 1264–1272

Loehle C, McCulloch JH (2008a) A 2000-Year Global Temperature Reconstruction Based On Non-Tree Ring Proxies. Energy & Environment, Vol 18, No 7&8

Loehle C, McCulloch JH (2008b) Correction to: A 2000-Year Global Temperature Reconstruction Based On Non-Tree Ring Proxies. Energy & Environment, Vol 19, No 1

Lomborg B (2016) Impact of current climate proposals. Glob Policy 7:109–118. doi:10.1111/1758-5899.12295

Luthi D, Le Floch M, Bereiter B, Blunier T, Barnola JM, Siegenthaler U, Raynaud D, Jouzel J, Fischer H, Kawamura K, Stocker TF (2008) High-resolution carbon dioxide concentration record 650,000 – 800,000 years before present. Nature, Vol. 453, pp. 379–382, 15 May 2008. doi:10.1038/nature06949

Madhu M, Hatfield JL (2015) Elevated carbon dioxide and soil moisture on early growth response of soybean. Agric Sci 6(2)

MAGICC – Model for the Assessment of Greenhouse Gas – Induced Climate Change, https://www.cato.org/carbon-tax-temperature-savings-calculator

Maibach E, Perkins D, Francis Z et al (2016) A 2016 national survey of American Meteorological Society member views on climate change: initial findings. Center for Climate Communication, George Mason University, Fairfax, VA, USA

Mann ME, Bradley RS, Hughes MK (1998) Global-scale temperature patterns and climate forcing over the past six centuries NATURE Vol 392

Mann ME, Bradley RS, Hughes MK (1999) Northern Hemisphere Temperatures during the Past Millenium: Inferences, Uncertainties, and Limitations. Geophysical Research Letters, Vol. 26, No. 6, pp 759–762

Mann ME, Jones PD (2003), Global surface temperatures over the past two millennia, Geophys. Res. Lett., 30, 1820, doi: 10.1029/2003GL017814, 15.

Marland G, Boden TA, Andres RJ (2008) Global, regional and national fossil fuel CO_2 emissions. In: Trends—a compendium of data on global change. CDIAC, Oak Ridge Nat Lab, U.S. Dept of Energy, Oak Ridge, TN, U.S.A.

Maue R (2016) Atlantic Basin Power Dissipation Index from HURDAT2, after Michaels

Maue R (2017) Global Tropical Cyclone Activity Weather Bell Models http://models.weatherbell.com/tropical.php

McAdie CJ, Landsea CW, Neumann CJ, David JE, and Blake ES (2009) Tropical Cyclones of the North Atlantic Ocean, 1851 – 2006 NOAA National Hurricane Center, National Climatic Data Center, Asheville, NC

Melillo JM, Richmond TC, Yohe GW, Eds (2014) Climate Change Impacts in the United States: The Third National Climate Assessment. U.S. Global Change Research Program, 841 pp. doi:10.7930/J0Z31WJ2.

Met Office Hadley Centre observations datasets, accessed March, 2017 http://www.metoffice.gov.uk/hadobs/hadcrut4/data/current/download.html

Michaels P, Balling RC, Hutzler MJ, Davis RE, Knappenberger PC, Idso CD (2012) Addendum: Global Climate Change Impacts in the United States, Center For The Study Of Science Cato Institute

Michaels P., Knappenberger PC (2015) Lukewarming The new climate science that changes everything. CATO Institute, 1000 Massachusetts Avenue, NW, Washington, DC 20001

Moore TG (1996) Warmer is Richer, Hoover Institution Stanford University https://web.stanford.edu/~moore/HistoryEcon.html

Moore P (2016) The dangerous 150-million-year decline in CO_2. Frontier Inst, Toronto, Canada.

Morice CP, Kennedy JJ, Rayner NA, Jones PD (2012) Quantifying uncertainties in global and regional temperature change using an ensemble of observational estimates: The HadCRUT4 dataset, J. Geophysical. Res., 117, D08101, doi: 10.1029/2011JD017187.

Mörner N-A (2011) Setting the frames of expected future sea level changes by exploring past geological sea level records. Chapter 6 of book, D Easterbrook, Evidence-Based Climate Science, 2011 Elsevier B.V. ISBN: 978-0-12-385956-3

Myers, N (2005) Environmental refugees, an emergent security issue', 13. Economic forum, Prague, OSCE, May 2005, Millennium Ecosystem Assessment, 2005

Narisma GT, Foley JA, Licker R et al (2007) Abrupt changes in rainfall during the 20th century. Geophys Res Lett 34(6), doi:10.1029/2006GL028628

NASA (2016) Carbon Dioxide Fertilization Greening Earth, Study Finds, https://www.nasa.gov/feature/goddard/2016/carbon-dioxide-fertilization-greening-earth, accessed 3/13/17; permission R. Myneni

National Integrated Drought Information System, US Drought Portal https://www.drought.gov/drought/

NIFC (2017) National Interagency Fire Center - Total Wildland Fires and Acres (1960 – 2015), https://www.nifc.gov/fireInfo/fireInfo_stats_totalFires.html, accessed 04/2017

National Weather Service, snowfall history Pittsburgh, PA https://www.weather.gov/media/pbz/records/hissnow.pdf

NOAA Technical Memorandum NWS NHC-6, USGCRP National Climate Assessment (2014) Adapted from Kossin et al (2007)

NOAA (2016) NWS Storm Prediction Center. US Annual Trends of Local Storm Reports Tornadoes http://www.spc.noaa.gov/wcm/2016/torngraph-big.png

NOAA (2017a) U.S. percentage areas very wet/very dry. https://www.ncdc.noaa.gov/temp-and-precip/uspa/wet-dry/10, accessed 2017 May 2

NOAA (2017a) National Center for Environment—US Tornado Climatology. Regions of the World with Increased Likelihood of Experiencing Tornadoes, https://www.ncdc.noaa.gov/climate-information/extreme-events/us-tornado-climatology

NOAA (2017b) NOAA NCEI Historical Records and Trends, https://www.ncdc.noaa.gov/climate-information/extreme-events/us-tornado-climatology/trends

NOAA (2017c) NOAA National Weather Service Enhanced Fujita Scale, https://www.weather.gov/oun/tornadodata-okc-appendix

NOAA PMEL (2017) Hawaii Carbon Dioxide Time-Series. https://www.pmel.noaa.gov/co2/file/Hawaii+Carbon+Dioxide+Time-Series

Noon (2016) What if Obama's climate change policies are based on pHraud? CFact post http://www.cfact.org/2014/12/22/what-if-obamas-climate-change-policies-are-based-on-phraud/#sthash.XQXdXjvE.dpuf

Oerlemans J (2005) Extracting a Climate Signal from 169 Glacier Records. *Science* 29 Apr 2005: Vol. 308, Issue 5722, pp. 675–677 DOI: 10.1126/science.1107046

Oregon Petition (2008) http://petitionproject.com

Oreskes, N (2004) The scientific consensus on climate change. Science 306, 1686

Overdieck D, Reid C, Strain BR (1988) The effects of pre-industrial and future CO_2 concentrations on growth, dry matter production and the carbon-nitrogen relationship in plants at low nutrient supply: *Vigna unguiculata* (Cowpea), *Abelmoschus esculentus* (Orka) and *Raphinus sativus* (Radish). Angewandte Botanik 62:119–134.

Owen J, (2009) Sahara Desert Greening Due to Climate Change? National Geographic News, July 2009

Parker DE, Legg TP, Folland CK (1992) A new daily Central England Temperature Series, 1772 – 1991. Int. J. Clim., Vol 12, pp 317–342, www.metoffice.gov.uk/hadobs.

Pelejero C, Calvo E, McCulloch MT, Marshall JF, Gagan MK, Lough JM, Opdyke BN (2005), Preindustrial to Modern Interdecadal Variability in Coral Reef pH, Science 309, 2204, 2005

PSMSL (2008) Permanent Service for Mean Sea Level. Recent global sea level acceleration started over 200 years ago? http://www.psmsl.org/products-/reconstructions/gslGRL2008.txt

Rohde R (2017) Global Warming Art

Robinson GD and Robinson GD (2012) Global Warming—Alarmists, Skeptics, and Deniers. Moonshine Publishing, Abbeville, SC

Rode KD (2013) Spatial and temporal variation in polar bear responses to sea ice loss: Powerpoint presentation to Alaska Sea Grant Conference, College of Fisheries and Ocean Sciences University of Alaska Fairbanks

Rode KD, Regehr EV, Douglas D et al (2014) Variation in the response of an Arctic top predator experiencing habitat loss: feeding and reproductive ecology of two polar bear populations. Global Change Biology 20:76–88, doi:10.1111/gcb.12339

Rojo-Garibaldi B, Salas-d-Leon DA, Sánchez NL, Monreal-Gómez MA (2016) Hurricanes in the Gulf of Mexico and the Caribbean Sea and their relationship with sunspots Journal of Atmospheric and Solar-Terrestrial Physics 148 · October 2016 DOI: 10.1016/j.jastp.2016.08.007

Ross T and Lott N (2003) A Climatology of 1980 – 2003 Extreme Weather and Climate Events, NOAA, National Climatic Data Center Technical Report No. 2003-1

Rutgers University Global Snow Lab http://climate.rutgers.edu/snowcover

Schott T, Landsea C, Hafele G, Lorens G, Taylor A, Thurm H, Ward B, Willis M, and Zaleski W (2012) Saffir-Simpson Hurricane Wind Scale, NOAA National Hurricane Center

Schulte K-M (2008) Scientific consensus on climate change? Energy Environ 19(2).

Scotese CR (2002) Analysis of the temperature oscillations in geological eras. Paleomap Project http://www.scotese.com/climate.htm

Seaquist JW, Hickler T, Eklundh L, Ardö J, and Heumann, (2009) Disentangling the effects of climate and people on Sahel vegetation dynamics, Biogeosciences, 6, 469–477, doi:10.5194/bg-6-469-2009, 2009.

Segelastad T (2008) Carbon Isotope Mass Balance Modelling of Atmospheric vs. Oceanic CO_2. 33rd International Geological Congress (Session TC), Oslo, Norway 6 – 14 August 2008

Spencer R (2017) UAH Satellite-Based Temperature of the Global Lower Atmosphere (Version 6.0), http://www.drroyspencer.com/latest-global-temperatures/

Springmann M, Mason-D'Croz D, Robinson S, Garnett T, Godfray HC, Gollin D, Rayner M, Ballon P, Scarborough P (2016) Global and regional health effects of future food production under climate change: a modelling study. Lancet 2016, May 7, 387:1937–46, doi: 10.1016/S0140-6736(15)01156-3

Stein M (2015) A Disgrace to the Profession. Stockade Books, Woodsville, NH

Swann AL, Swann S, Hoffman FM et al (2016) Plant responses to increasing CO_2 reduce estimates of climate impacts on drought severity. PNAS113(36):10019-10024

Tans P, Keeling R, (2017) Trends in Atmospheric Carbon Dioxide. Earth System Research Laboratory (ESRL), Global Monitoring Division, NOAA https://www.esrl.noaa.gov/gmd/ccgg/trends/data.html

Tol R (2015) Global warming consensus claim does not stand up. The Australian, (author's cut) http://richardtol.blogspot.com/2015/03/now-almost-two-years-old-john-cooks-97.html

UAH Global Temperature Update (2017) National Space Science and Technology Center (NSSTC) The University of Alabama in Huntsville http://www.nsstc.uah.edu/data/msu/v6.0/tlt/uahncdc_lt_6.0.txt

U. K. Office for National Statistics (2017) Excess winter mortality in England and Wales: 2015/16 (provisional) and 2014/15 (final) https://www.ons.gov.uk/peoplepopulationandcommunity/birthsdeathsand-marriages/deaths/bulletins/excesswintermortalityinenglandandwales/2015to2016provisionaland2014to2015final

United Nations Environment Programme (2005) Environmental refugees, An emergent security issue, 13. Econom. Original map has been removed from website, archived document available here: https://wattsup-withthat.files.wordpress.com/2011/04/un_50million_11kap9climat.png

UNFAO (2012) United Nations Food and Agriculture Organization: World grain production 1961-2012. Food Outlook, May 2012, p. 1

UNFAO (2017) United Nations Food and Agriculture Organization: http://www.fao.org/faostat/en/#compare

University of Missouri Corn Extension, accessed May 2017. https://plantsciences.missouri.edu/grains/corn/facts.htm

USDA (2017) World Agricultural Outlook Board, World agricultural supply and demand estimates updated to February.

US Global Change Research Program (2009) Global climate change impacts in the United States. Cambridge University Press, Cambridge

US National Weather Service (2017) The Atmosphere. NOAA http://www.srh.noaa.gov/jetstream/atmos/atmos_intro.html

USEIA (2017) Frequently asked questions: How much CO_2 is produced when different fuels are burned? US Energy Information Administration Accessed 5/20/17 at https://www.eia.gov/tools/faqs/faq.php?id=73&t=11

Vardoulakis S, Dear K, Hajat S, Heaviside C, Eggen B, McMichael AJ (2014) Comparative Assessment of the Effects of Climate Change on Heat- and Cold-Related Mortality in the United Kingdom and Australia, Environmental Health Perspectives, volume 122, number 12

Waelbroeck C, Labeyrie L, Michel E, Duplessy JC, McManus J, Lambeck K, Balbon E, and Labracherie M (2002) Sea-level and deep water temperature changes derived from benthic foraminifera isotopic records. Quaternary Science Reviews, Vol. 21, pp. 295-305.

Watson, P.J., 2011. Is There Evidence Yet of Acceleration in Mean Sea Level Rise around Mainland Australia? *Journal of Coastal Research*, 27(2), 368-377.

Will G (2009) The Truth About Global Warming. Newsweek 11/6/2009, http://www.newsweek.com/george-will-truth-about-global-warming-76899

Yang, J, Tian H, Tao B, Ren W, Kush J, Liu Y, and Wang Y (2014) Spatial and temporal patterns of global burned area in response to anthropogenic and environmental factors: Reconstructing global fire history for the 20th and early 21st centuries, J Geophys Res Biogeosci, 119, 249 263, doi:10.1002/2013JG002532.

York J, Dowsley M, Cornwell A et al (2016) Demographic and traditional knowledge perspectives on the current status of Canadian polar bear subpopulations, Ecol Evol, 6:2897–2924,p doi:10.1002/ece3.2030

Zachos J, Pagani M, Sloan L, Thomas E, Billups K (2001) Trends, Rhythms, and Aberrations in Global Climate 65 Ma to Present. Science 27 Apr 2001: Vol. 292, Issue 5517, pp. 686-693 DOI: 10.1126/science.1059412

Zachos JC, Ro U, Schellenberg SA, Sluijs A, Hodell DA Kelly DC, Thomas E, Nicolo M, Raffi I, Lourens LJ, McCarren H, Kroon D (2005) Rapid Acidification of the Ocean During the Paleocene-Eocene Thermal Maximum, Science, Vol 308 pp 1611-1615

Zhu Z, et al. (2016) Greening of the Earth and its drivers, Nature Climate Change 6, 791–795